THE SOCIETY OF BIBLICAL LITERATURE
SEMEIA STUDIES
Lou H. Silberman, Editor

PAUL AND THE IRONY OF AFFLICT

PAUL AND THE
IRONY OF AFFLICTION

Karl A. Plank

SCHOLARS PRESS
Atlanta, Georgia

PAUL AND THE IRONY OF AFFLICTION

Library of Congress Cataloging in Publication Data

Plank, Karl A. (Karl Andrews)
   Paul and the irony of affliction.

   (Semeia studies)
   Bibliography: p.
   1. Bible. N.T. Corinthians, 1st IV, 9-13--Criticism, interpretation,
etc. 2. Suffering--Biblical teaching. 3. Irony in the Bible. 4. Paul, the
Apostle, Saint. I. Title. II. Series.
BS2675.2.P52   1987   227.2066   87-4844
   ISBN 1-55540-102-3 (alk. paper)
        1-55540-103-1 (pbk. : alk. paper)

Printed in the United States of America
on acid-free paper

In memoriam

Charles Andrews Plank
1896–1986

ACKNOWLEDGMENTS

This study is a revision of a doctoral dissertation completed at Vanderbilt University in 1983. While I hope the present version has overcome the stigmata of its origins, I yet remain grateful to those teachers who nurtured its beginnings and have helped me sustain its growth: Paul W. Meyer, Daniel Patte (who directed the dissertation), Mary Ann Tolbert, John R. Donahue, S.J. and Gerd Luedemann. Also I am indebted to R. David Kaylor and Wm. Trent Foley for their friendship at Davidson and their counsel on matters ranging from the convictions of Paul to the mysteries of the computer. And lastly, I want to thank Lou H. Silberman, not only for the influence of his teaching, but for his particular guidance in the preparation of this study for publication.

Family and close companions are nearer to these pages than they may know and I can tell.

Karl A. Plank
Davidson, North Carolina
St. Wilfrid of York, 1986

TABLE OF CONTENTS

Chapter I

A POETIC PAUL AND THE LANGUAGE OF AFFLICTION

He is neither priest nor proctor at low eve.

WALLACE STEVENS, "An Ordinary Evening
in New Haven"

PAUL, A KIND OF POET

Paul writes as "a kind of poet."[1] Through a keen use of language the apostle reveals his literary artistry, especially in the Corinthian correspondence. There every concession of inept speech pales before his control of pattern and image. Every protest of ineloquence bows to the force of his masterful irony and paradox. Apart from whatever else may describe his activity in the Corinthians letters, Paul's powerful manipulation of symbolic speech[2] marks him as kin to the poet and literary artist.

To speak of a poetic Paul is to grant integrity to his writing and recognize that his language does not so much ornament his gospel as become part of its fabric. For critics to approach Paul as poet, to read his letters from the vantage point of literary criticism, encourages a particular interest on their part: namely, to read with an eye sensitive to the way in which his symbolic language discloses deep convictions, engages his readers in their sense of self, and creates a unity with the message it would express.

[1] The category, "a kind of poet," is taken from Louis Mackey's insightful discussion of Kierkegaard. See Mackey ix-xiii.

[2] "Symbolic speech" refers to the use of language to emphasize the connotative dimensions of discourse as opposed to the denotative emphasis of "plain speech". Where "plain speech" functions to communicate information with clarity, "symbolic speech" draws on ambiguity and tension to engage the reader's imagination and awaken his or her vision of life. On "symbolic speech" see Daniel Patte and Aline Patte 2–3 and Robert Tannehill 11–28.

Admittedly, Paul writes only as a *kind* of poet. Unlike the artists who offer their work for aesthetic contemplation, Paul uses poetic language in the Corinthian letters to serve given demands: to vindicate his authority, to restore relationship between himself and the Corinthians, to promote a different orientation to life and the actions which follow from it—broadly to proclaim his gospel and encourage its reception. As such, Paul writes as a *rhetorical* poet, addressing his language to a specific audience and circumstance.[3] As a rhetorical poet Paul's language bears the impress of a particular situation even as it creates aesthetic unity. Through its rhetorical features Paul's language seeks to become "a word on target in the midst of human historical specificity" (Beker, 1978:142), a word fully poetic in its power and integrity, but distinctly situational in its address and intention.

Notwithstanding the increasing surge of literary-critical perspectives in biblical studies, the notion of a poetic Paul—even a rhetorical one—may yet sound strange to the ear attuned to other resonances. The legacy of Pauline interpretation shows a decidedly theological and historical tendency, a persistent interest in discerning the content of Paul's faith and the cultural context of his ministry. The literary tack, however, does not depart from that legacy as much as reformulate what its interest might entail. A poetic Paul is no less a theologian, only a theologian of a different stripe. As theologian, the poetic Paul does not reflect at distance about the reality of God, but employs symbolic language to re-present that reality in the world of his readers.[4] Consequently, to understand the convictions which characterize Paul's faith,[5] theologically-motivated critics can-

---

[3] Following the work of Chaim Perelman (1969 and 1982), "rhetoric" here refers to the use of language to facilitate a "contact of minds." It is discourse which intends to influence and effect a given audience or state of affairs. As such, rhetoric is characterized in terms of its *function* (what the language does) and its *situation* (the context within which a speaker or writer engages an audience).

[4] In this respect the Jesus of the parables exists as the literary precursor of the poetic Paul. Thus, Robert Funk: "If the parable is that mode of language which founds a world, and that particular world under the domain of God's grace, all other language in the Christian tradition is derivative in relation to it. It is out of this 'poetic' medium that the tradition springs, however far in fact it may subsequently wander from it. Paul's language, as well as other languages in the New Testament and early church, presupposes such a foundational language tradition" (244). Note also Sallie McFague's discussion of Paul as an "intermediary theologian," a theologian whose mode of discourse is consonant with the parables of Jesus (157–62).

[5] The notion of "conviction" here and throughout the study refers to that which is perceived as self-evidently true. In contrast with "ideas" which are mediated

not avoid the literary dimensions of his writing, *how* his faith becomes a reality in the world of God's calling which he re-presents and shares with the Corinthians.

Nor is a poetic Paul any less of an historical figure. Like his or her historically-inclined predecessor, the literary critic may remain interested in the historical Paul, the contours of his ministry, and the cultural influences that shaped his activity. However, this same critic will refuse to construe Paul's letters as any form of clear glass through which he or she might directly glimpse the apostle and his world. The writings of a poetic Paul have a density that deflects historical reconstruction and allows the apostle to remain elusive at least until the critic comes to terms with the literary character of the texts which imply his portrait. Accordingly, to speak of a poetic Paul does not banish his letters from the domain of history, but suggests instead that they provide historical evidence only in an indirect, oblique manner. To recover the portrait of Paul, the historical critics must first discern the way Paul's letters continually mediate and shape the voice for which they listen.

In this study we take up the notion of Paul as a rhetorical poet in order to understand a specific instance of discourse, his self-description of affliction in 1 Cor. 4:9–13. Our thesis, put simply, is that Paul's language of affliction here embodies a thorough and fundamental irony. The literary vantage point from which we engage Paul allows us to discern and display this irony. Moreover, it leads us to observe the particular function of his language of affliction within 1 Corinthians 1–4 and to identify the underlying convictions which characterize that discourse. To know the rhetorical function of Paul's language of affliction clarifies how Paul understood the Corinthian situation and thus illumines the context of his ministry; to discern the convictions inflected by that language suggests how Paul envisioned reality and thus grants insight into the nature of his theology.

PAUL AND THE LANGUAGE OF AFFLICTION

Paul draws upon a language of affliction in virtually all his letters to interpret human life and the gospel he understands to empower that life. With this language he creates a textual world in which

through demonstration and yield knowledge, "convictions" grow from the imagination's vision of life and issue in belief. They are the fundamental assumptions which shape an individual's thought, speech, and discernment of reality. As such, they express an individual's faith. On "conviction" see Patte 1983: 10–27.

suffering persists and weakness characterizes the human lot. The world to which Paul lures his readers shows its messiah to be a crucified lord, his apostles to be "afflicted in every way" (2 Cor. 4:8) and human communities to endure those same sufferings (2 Cor. 1:5–7). Although not a world without affirmation, Paul's "groaning creation" (Rom. 8:22) nevertheless finds comfort only in the midst of affliction, in the context of tribulation which Paul highlights as the most salient feature of worldly life.

Study of Paul's language of affliction takes us close to his deepest convictions, those truths which he assumes to be self-evident and which shape his perception and understanding of human life. Through this language he speaks about himself, his vocation, and the God who calls him to be an apostle. With its use he allows us to detect the lens through which he sees life and its reality. The study of virtually any aspect of Paul's theology must eventually consider this language, not because of its abundance as much as its fundamental character. Deeply enmeshed in the fabric of his gospel and his way of seeing the world, the language of affliction does not provide simply another theological topic in the Pauline compendium. Rather, it exposes the ground on which the apostle does theology.

Nowhere does the language of affliction have greater prominence than in the Corinthian correspondence. There the converging vectors of Paul's cross theology, his own experience of weakness, and his perception of a Corinthian world-alienation place the language of affliction at the center of controversy. Throughout the correspondence this language participates in the persisting conflict over Paul's authority and the nature of the Corinthian calling—a conflict which, at every turn, calls into question the power and implication of his gospel.

Markedly theological, Paul's language of affliction readily lends itself to thematic description. However, in the Corinthian letters, this language signifies more than words whose content concerns adversity, suffering, and weakness. It signifies, in addition, a grammar, a syntax—a "way of speaking". As we will show, that "way of speaking" in 1 Cor. 4:9–13 is utterly ironic, creating a playful structure of discourse that sets into motion interacting perspectives of appearance and reality. Moreover, Paul's ironic language also has a particular rhetorical function or effect on his audience. Through irony Paul riddles his readers' fundamental orientation toward reality and thus begins a subterranean assault on the problematic Corinthian sensibility. Paul's language intends to shake the foundations on which the Corinthians have constructed their world and thus to undermine the ground from which have grown their objections to his apostleship and their own calling. As a "way of speaking" and as a "function" or "effect," the language of affliction manifests *poetic* and *rhetorical* dimensions that invite us to listen not only to *what* Paul says, but *how* he says it and what it *does* as it is spoken. In focussing upon an instance of this language we will study these dimensions in detail, seeking to identify their interrelationship and the way they work together to create a meaningful text.

Past research into Paul's language of affliction has shown a certain stylistic and rhetorical interest, focussing primarily on the catalogs of adversity or the so-called "peristasis catalogs".[6] In this respect our present work does not mark a new interest as much as modify and reconceive a trajectory already begun in the pioneering study of Weiss (1897) and the 1910 dissertation of his pupil, Bultmann. However, the differences between the earlier studies and our own criticism of 1 Cor. 4:9–13 yet run deep and reflect a new direction in focussing upon the rhetoric of Paul's irony.

Previous studies of Paul's "peristasis catalogs", although diverse, have tended to share a common concern for the textual *background*. Weiss, Bultmann, and their followers investigated the language and style of Paul's writings, but primarily as indices to determine the apostle's cultural background. Bultmann, for example, noted the stylistic similarities between Epictetus' enumeration of Stoic adversities (e.g., I.11.33 and I.18.22) and the apostle's listing of comparable afflictions (Bultmann 19 and 71) and thereby continued to build his case for Paul's cultural affinity with Hellenistic writers.

Such studies have made careful observations of Paul's rhetoric, but in doing so have tended to abstract the apostle's language from its literary context, separating it from its immediate constraints in the discourse of a given letter. Within the parameters of these studies Paul's language bears no intrinsic interest. Its function within a particular correspondence or its symbolic evocation appears

---

[6] Along with 1 Cor. 4:9–13 critics usually include as the so-called "peristasis catalogs" 2 Cor. 4:7–10; 6:3–10; 11:23–27; 12:10; Rom. 8:35; and Phil. 4:11–13. For early critical study of Paul's rhetoric including the catalogs of adversity see Weiss (1897), Bultmann, and Farrar (1879 and 1885). On the catalogs themselves see the respective works of Fridrichsen (1928; 1929; 1944), Schrage, Zmijewski, and Fitzgerald. In addition to rhetorical and stylistic studies, there exists a wealth of theological and exegetical research; see especially E. Guettgemanns.

to make no significant difference to the controlling question of cultural affinity. In this perspective Paul's language takes on an artifactual character. The relic of another time and place, Paul's rhetoric here beckons the critic not to linger on the meaning of the language itself or the letters in which it exists, but to see through it to the cultural forces that contributed to its shape.

Our own study focuses not on the cultural *background* which may shape Paul's language of affliction, but on the textual *foreground* which that language creates. As the artifact of a given time and place Paul's rhetoric bears a history and reflects the cultural constraints of its original production. A world exists behind Paul's language which the historian may approach with rigorous criticism. At the same time, however, once the apostle's language becomes inscribed in a text, his rhetoric assumes a certain distance from its origins and takes on a textual autonomy free from the constraints of the author's intention and world.[7] If Paul's speech reflects a world behind him, 1 Corinthians 1–4 yet projects a world in front of the text, a mode of being which "the work unfolds, discovers, reveals" (Ricoeur 1981:143).[8] Where the historical critic probes the cultural background for the origins of Paul's language of affliction, our present literary study seeks to penetrate the textual foreground to observe the world which Paul's text constructs and which its readers inhabit in their act of reading.

Concentrating on the textual foreground encourages the critic to understand rhetorical discourse more as an on-going event than as an artifact. The historical Paul, as writer, gives birth to 1 Corinthians

[7] Here I follow the theoretical research of Paul Ricoeur, in particular his discussion of the phenomenon of distanciation. In distinguishing speaking from writing Ricoeur notes how the latter renders a text autonomous with respect to the author's intention and world. Once inscribed, the meaning of a text is set at distance from the original constraints of discourse and liberated from the history of its enunciation. On distanciation see Ricoeur 1976: 25–45 and 1981: 131–144.

[8] That texts project to their readers a world, a mode of being "in front of" the text, is a fundamental axiom in Ricoeur's interpretation theory (and a corollary of his notion of distanciation). Thus he writes of textual appropriation, "Ultimately, what I appropriate is a proposed world. The latter is not *behind* the text, as a hidden intention would be, but *in front of* it, as that which the work unfolds, discovers, reveals. Henceforth, to understand is *to understand oneself in front of the text*. It is not a question of imposing upon the text our finite capacity of understanding, but of exposing ourselves to the text and receiving from it an enlarged self, which would be the proposed existence corresponding in the most suitable way to the world proposed." (1981:143; also see 182–193 and 1976: 36–37).

1–4 but upon completing that task surrenders control of its meaning to the reader. The relation between the historical author and the completed text is a dead one: to pose the issue of Paul's rhetoric in terms of that relation inevitably entombs the language of affliction as an artifact in the Pauline reliquary. But if the critic looks instead to the interplay between text and reader—what occurs when the reader enters the world projected by the text—then Paul's rhetoric becomes alive, thriving in the process of reading. In the discourse of 1 Corinthians Paul's language of affliction makes something happen: readers change or bear the scars of resisting change. Such an event occurs in the textual foreground and, at least in part, constitutes the *function* of Paul's rhetoric and the meaning of his language of affliction.

A METHODOLOGICAL PRESCRIPT

To speak of literary and rhetorical methods in the context of our study is, to a certain extent, artificial. As we have used it, literary and rhetorical criticism refers to no clear set of procedures—method per se—but exists as a "field-encompassing-field" and, as such, includes a wide variety of critical operations.[9] Literary and rhetorical criticism provides here a methodological paradigm that furnishes a framework of basic commitments and presuppositions within which we approach our text.

In contrast to the historical paradigm which has dominated New Testament exegesis since the Enlightenment, the literary-rhetorical paradigm is essentially linguistically-based and systemic in character.[10] As *linguistically-based,* the paradigm affirms language as a fundamental category: the language of a text does not grant access to some reality behind or beyond its own expression, but refers to the reality of its own creation. As *systemic,* the paradigm insists that a text's meaning does not emerge genetically in terms of its development or cause, but as created synchronically within a textual system of relations. The literary-rhetorical paradigm is not exhausted by these dimensions, nor does it have sole claim to them.

[9] On the notion of "field-encompassing-field" see Van Harvey 54–59.
[10] For consideration of the historical paradigm note Van Harvey 38–101 and Edgar Krentz. For further discussion of the contrast between literary and historical paradigms as it pertains to biblical studies, see Patte 1976: 1–20; Petersen 9–23; and Hans Frei's extensive study, *The Eclipse of Biblical Narrative.*

However, they do reflect the most fundamental characteristics of the paradigm in its current practice.

The particular shape that the literary-rhetorical paradigm has taken in this study has been informed by several sources of theoretical research: the hermeneutical theory of Paul Ricoeur,[11] the "New Rhetoric" of Chaim Perelman,[12] phenomenology of reading and reader-response criticism,[13] and structural linguistics.[14] The theoretical contributions of this research combine in a complementary way within the literary-rhetorical paradigm. At a basic level of agreement, these sources share a general commitment to the model of a literary text as a form of communication: the meaning of a text occurs through the interaction of an author, text, and reader, comparable to the interaction of sender, message, and receiver that governs the act of communication.[15] Each of these theoretical sources may emphasize to a different degree the author, text, or reader, yet all resist the separation of one component from another and contribute to the evolving definition of these terms.

Here our concern has been only to sketch a methodological orientation and to make some reference to pertinent literature where questions of method are treated more extensively. To complete this prescript we acknowledge five assumptions operative

[11] Note especially Ricoeur's discussions of textuality, distanciation, and appropriation. See Ricoeur 1981 and also 1970 and 1977.
[12] Perelman's work provides philosophical reflection on the nature of rhetoric as argumentation and insists that, through the speaker's perceptions, it is always audience-specific and situation-bound. The manifesto of the "New Rhetoric" is Perelman's volume, *The New Rhetoric*, co-authored with L. Olbrechts-Tyteca; also note, Perelman 1982 and 1979. For critical exposition of Perelman's work see the respective works of Zyskind and Dempster.
[13] Audience-oriented criticisms such as phenomenology of reading and reader-response criticism highlight the ways in which a reader participates in the creation of a text's meaning and illumine the affective and pragmatic functions of literary language. On the literature generally, note respectively Suleiman and Crosman, Tompkins, Fish (1980), and Bleich; and on phenomenology of reading specifically, note Iser 1975 and 1978.
[14] Our emphasis on the convictional dimensions of Paul's text is nurtured primarily by structural and semiotic research. For a general overview of this literature, see the respective works of Scholes, Hawkes, and Wittig; more specifically note Greimas and Courtes. As applied to biblical exegesis, see Daniel Patte 1976 and Daniel Patte and Aline Patte, *Structural Exegesis: From Theory to Practice*.
[15] The communication model is commonly associated with the work of Roman Jakobson. See e.g., Jakobson, "Closing Statement: Linguistics and Poetics".

throughout this study. Emerging from the theoretical research noted above, they focus primarily on the components of the communication model and attempt to say what we mean by "author," "text," and "reader."

1. As inscribed discourse, a *text* implies an author and a reader and projects a world in which they interact. That world, which the text symbolizes, does not exist "behind" the text but, as a textual reality, is perpetually in the process of being disclosed through its reading. At its depths, the textual world creates and expresses a system of value that indicates the author's fundamental convictions.

2. The *author* whose convictions the text reveals exists first of all as a textual reality and does not grant *direct* access to the intentions of the historical author who put "pen to paper." When we refer to Paul or the apostle, we have in mind the Paul created by 1 Corinthians, the implied author whose voice speaks in the text, whose convictions coincide with its underlying values, and whose intentions are illumined by "the core of norms and choices" (Booth 1961:74) which it presupposes.

3. The *reader,* like the implied author, exists as a fictional inhabitant of the text and should be distinguished from the "individual upon whose crossed knee rests the open volume." (Gibson 2) As intended or ideal readers Paul's audience is defined through his perception of their values and situation; their role is created by the decisions and strategies which he implements. The "Corinthian reader" resides not in ancient Corinth, but in the world of 1 Corinthians. There they appear, not of their own volition, but through what Paul directly says about them and through what his own rhetoric presupposes of their situation.

4. Author and reader share a *rhetorical situation* which the text brings into view. Constituted by the author's perception of him- or herself and the audience, the rhetorical situation reflects the relationship between them and frequently can be understood in terms of some exigency which the discourse poses and addresses. As with the implied author and reader, the rhetorical situation exists as a textual reality.

5. The *rhetorical effect* refers to the particular changes and affects which the author would incite in the readers as they progress through the text. Taken broadly, the rhetorical effect is the possible actualization of the text which the author intends to promote in the reader. In this sense, the rhetorical effect coincides with the commitments summoned in the serious reception of the discourse.

OVERVIEW

This study focuses upon Paul's ironic language of affliction in 1 Cor. 4:9–13. In particular, it seeks to understand the rhetorical situation of Paul's language of affliction (chapter 2), how his irony functions in that situation and what convictions it expresses (chapter 3), and the rhetoric and style which forcefully implement those convictions (chapter 4). Our contention is that through a rhetoric of irony Paul's language of affliction meets the apologetic and homiletic demands of the discourse and creates a paradoxical world for his readers. More than a textual strategy, the paradoxical irony of 1 Corinthians 1–4 characterizes the way Paul sees the world and his deepest convictions of the gospel.

Chapter II

THE RHETORICAL SITUATION OF
1 CORINTHIANS 1–4

> Persons are rightly suspicious when they are called only
> to joy.
>
> LISTON MILLS
> "The Self as Helmsman"

Literary and rhetorical criticisms seek to illumine the interaction of textual part and whole. Over against the legacy of piecemeal reading—habits of interpretation that sever given bits of text from their relationship with other portions of a common text—the literary or the rhetorical critic emphasizes the vital role of textual context in discerning the meaning of any given passage. No portion of text bears meaning in general, but only in terms of some context which locates it in a specific sphere of discourse. In context, the meaning of a text becomes perceptible and particular. Yet not just any context will suffice. For the literary or rhetorical critic, a portion of text is first of all a textual reality, shaped and enriched by its place within a larger textual whole. The interaction between that whole and part reveals the underlying values of the world which the text creates. It maps the textual foreground and obligates the critical reader to take seriously the full dimensions of literary context.

Paul's description of affliction (4:9–13) finds its immediate literary context within the opening discourse of 1 Corinthians (chs. 1–4). In this study we focus on these chapters as the larger context within which Paul's description reveals its function and meaning. We do so not to banish the rest of 1 Corinthians or the Corinthian correspondence from our view, but to begin the task of a contextual reading within a clear unit of discourse. While these chapters also have *their* place within 1 Corinthians, they yet provide a "whole" that interacts decisively with the "part," 4:9–13, and allow us, with some focus, to take the first steps toward a fuller literary understanding of our passage.

1 Corinthians 1–4 shows a rhetorical unity. Here Paul writes as a "rhetorical poet" using the language of affliction to climax a many-faceted argument. Under the pressure of community criticism, Paul would convince the Corinthians of his apostolic authority and, at the same time, bring about a change in their way of perceiving him, themselves, and the world they hold in common. Rhetoric, no attempt to coerce agreement, seeks a genuine "community of minds" through persuasion (Perelman and Olbrechts-Tyteca 14). It is a use of language which has a function and aims to *do* something within a given situation. A study of 1 Corinthians 1–4 allows us to understand more specifically what Paul aims to do as his language of affliction turns forcefully ironic in 4:9–13.

We find in 1 Corinthians 1–4 the rhetorical situation within which Paul's language of affliction has its function. A rhetorical situation has as its basic features a speaker's perception of him- or herself (in this case, the writer, Paul), of the audience (the Corinthians), and of the exigence they share.[1] The two-fold exigence we have suggested above—Paul's need to defend his apostleship and reorient the Corinthians—we will discuss as the *apologetic* and *homiletic* contexts of 1 Corinthians 1–4. Although speaker and audience mutually define each other in both contexts, the apologetic gives peculiar access to Paul's perception of himself in relation to the community; the homiletic to his perception of the community in relation to him.

THE APOLOGETIC CONTEXT   *not persuasive*

The work of Hans Dieter Betz on Galatians and his earlier monograph on 2 Corinthians 10–13 have given prominence to the category of "apologetic" in Pauline exegesis.[2] Betz shows that Paul directs much of his writing to a self-conscious effort to defend his authority against communal criticism and external opposition to his apostleship. In composing his apology or his defense, Betz argues, Paul draws upon traditional Greek rhetorical forms and models of

[1] On "rhetorical situation" see the respective works of Bitzer, Vatz, and Bormann.

[2] On Galatians, see Betz 1975 and 1979; on 2 Corinthians 10–13, see 1972. Note, too, Paul W. Meyer's review of Betz's *Galatians*, 1981.

organization and thus constructs his arguments in the genre of an "apologetic letter" (1979:14–15). Understood as genre, Betz's notion of apologetic becomes an idealized, formal type which facilitates comparison of Paul's writing with other "apologetic" texts, notably those of the Socratic tradition. But as genre, this view confines rhetoric within a strait jacket of "organization" and too easily excludes from consideration those texts whose apologetic *function* appears through diverse forms. Arguments with common intent often display similar form, but need not do so. Similar rhetorical goals can be pursued through a variety of forms that will vary relative to the speaker and audience and not simply to the desired end of the discourse (see Perelman and Olbrechts-Tyteca 142–43 and 490–502).

To identify apologetic discourse requires a rhetorical perspective sensitive to function as well as form and to the peculiar needs of apologetic argumentation. In terms of argumentation, apologetic discourse presupposes two basic elements: first, to engage in apologetic, speakers must perceive or anticipate a challenge against themselves or their actions; and second, that challenge, if unmet, must be sufficient to obstruct the performance of a chosen or required task. Apology is not idle discourse. It responds to a perceived criticism which the speaker cannot ignore without consequence.[3] Both of these markers of apologetic occur within 1 Corinthians 1–4.

The Contours of Criticism   weak
Corinthian Judgment (4:1–6)

The verses which frame Paul's appeal to apostolic suffering (4:9–13) suggest an accusatory setting and indicate that he perceives himself to be under Corinthian criticism. At 4:1 Paul resumes a line of argument begun in 3:5, a consideration of his own role and that of Apollos in the Corinthian community. Here Paul intensifies his language with a diction of judgment and evaluation: the pervasive repetition of *krinō* and its cognates (4:3–5); the requirement that a steward be deemed trustworthy (4:2); references to innocence and acquittal (4:4); and confident expressions of disclosure of intention

---

[3] Note that perceived criticism itself does not warrant apologetic response. The criticism needs to have a seriousness and magnitude that makes argumentation worthwhile, if not urgent. Inconsequential criticism is easier ignored. As Perelman and Olbrechts-Tyteca remind: "To engage in argument a person must attach some importance to gaining the adherence of his interlocutor, to securing his assent . . ." (16).

and commendation (4:5).[4] Through this language Paul protests his innocence and displaces the force of any alleged Corinthian indictment: the *kyrios* alone can judge the servant. The passage climaxes with a prohibition of human judgment which can only be premature until the Lord comes (4:5).[5] Taken together, the juridical imagery and Paul's intent to undercut the power of human judgment point to his perception of a challenge to his trustworthiness as an apostle.

Paul's Travel Plans (4:14–21)   *weak*

The text at 4:14–21 further indicates criticism against Paul. After exhorting the Corinthians to imitate him (4:16), Paul notes that certain of the Corinthians were acting arrogantly as if he were not coming to Corinth (4:18).[6] He replies strongly ("come to you I will!" 4:19) and threatens to turn his arrival into a power contest with his boastful detractors (4:19).

Paul's brevity obscures what is at stake in the criticism that he might not return to Corinth. Insofar as the issue continues, however, other portions of the Corinthian correspondence may suggest the contours of the present conflict. In 2 Cor. 1:15–2:4 Paul links his apparent failure to fulfill his travel plans with the issue of his integrity, the trustworthiness of his speech, and ultimately the reliability of his proclamation.

> Do I make my plans like a person of the world, ready to say yes and no at the same time? (I swear that as) God is trustworthy our word to you has not been yes and no. For the Son of God, Christ Jesus, the one whom we preached among you . . . was not yes and no; in him it is always yes. For all the promises of God find their yes in him. (2 Cor. 1:17–20)

Paul's antithesis between "word" and "power" (4:19,20) points to a further dimension. With a similar contrast Paul had already

[4] Paul's repetition of *anakrinō* (4:3–4) indicates most clearly the presence of criticism. The word evokes the imagery of the courtroom and judicial investigation of an accused person (cf. Acts 4:9; 12:19, 24:8; 28:18). Note, too, that in 1 Cor. 9:3 *anakrisis* occasions specifically *apologia*.

[5] Note that the syntax of the prohibition (*mē* plus the present imperative) implies that such judgment was already being expressed. See Blass and Debrunner #336.

[6] "*Ephusiōthēsan*," the verb Paul uses to express "acting arrogantly," provides a cognate echo with 4:6. Such arrogance is precisely what Paul hoped to end by rooting all judgment in eschatology.

described himself (2:4) and later in the correspondence alludes to the apparent criticism that his personal presence, including his speech, lacks the power that his letters imply from afar (2 Cor. 10:1,10). In the eyes of his critics, Paul cannot, in person, perform what the words of his letters would indicate at a distance. Here the issue of Paul's travel goes beyond his simple trustworthiness, whether or not he will return, and raises the question of the reasons for his absence. Does Paul delay his return because, in weakness, he is afraid to face the arrogant ones? Does the weakness of his presence imply the lack of power to fulfill his word?

Corinthian Groups (1:11–12 and 3:3–4)

In the report of Chloe's people, Paul learns of quarreling among the Corinthians, a dissension that he understands to involve grouping around various leaders (1:11–12) and to signify their immaturity in faith (3:3–4). We need not discuss here the numerous interpretations of the Corinthian parties.[7] For our purposes it is enough to note that the very existence of the groups implies a climate of criticism (cf. Perelman and Olbrechts-Tyteca 323). C.K. Barrett puts the matter this way:

> The existence of a "Paul group" itself implies opposition to Paul in Corinth. That some made a point of standing by the founder of the church shows that there were others who if they did not assail his position at least regarded him as *demode,* and preferred new missionaries. (43)

The existence of factions in Corinth confirms the likelihood of criticism directed against Paul but, in itself, does not specify the nature of that criticism.

Paul's Concession of Weakness *(1:15–17; 2:1–5; 3:1–4; 4:1–5, 9–13)*

As Nils Dahl has shown, at several key points of transition in 1 Corinthians 1–4 Paul refers back to his own ministry in Corinth (47). These references, as transitional devices, allow the argument to progress smoothly by mentioning a topic that Paul elaborates in the verses that follow (e.g., *sophia,* 1:17 and 2:5; Paul and Apollos, 3:4; premature judgment, 4:5). In addition, the content of these references points to an apologetic function. When he writes of his earlier activity in Corinth, Paul typically concedes some form of weakness

---

[7] On this question note Hurd 95–107, Conzelmann 33–34, Munck 135–67, and Vielhauer 341–52.

or limitation. He acknowledges that his commissioned purpose was neither to baptize nor to preach with eloquent wisdom (1:17); that his speech and proclamation lacked eloquence and wisdom and that, in Corinth, he was present with weakness, fear and trembling (2:1–5); that his address had not been one for the spiritually mature (3:1); and that humiliation and affliction characterized his apostleship (4:9–13). Paul does not concede his weakness out of simple candor. His admissions reflect accusations, either real or potential, and obstruct the effective use which others might make of his limitations. Concession, when used strategically, becomes a subtle mode of "anticipatory refutation" that reduces the force of an opponent's argument by conscripting it for one's own purposes (cf. Perelman 1969:501). Whether in response to actual accusation or to its anticipation, concession signals apologetic intent.

When Paul concedes weakness he admits the evidence against him but sets a trap for his opponents.[8] Once admitted, weakness testifies not against Paul, but on his behalf, as he redefines the whole notion within his paradox of the cross (1:18–25). Paul concedes the evidence only to challenge the criteria by which it is to be interpreted. Bringing weakness onto his own ground, Paul diminishes the significance of his accusers' objection to his limitations. Far from being an innocent admission, Paul's concession reflects the climate of accusation and a segment of his defense against Corinthian criticism.

The Apologetic Necessity

1 Corinthians 1–4 shows Paul to be under criticism and that criticism to concern generally his weakness, a vulnerability that includes the limitations of his speech and reliability as well as his physical presence. The second index of apologetic discourse looks to that criticism as being of sufficient substance and kind to require Paul's defense. Does the charge of weakness threaten Paul with consequences that he cannot ignore? If Paul fails to answer the Corinthian challenge, what has he lost?

---

[8] Cf. Perelman's discussion of concession: "Each time a speaker follows the interlocutor onto his own ground he makes a concession to him, but one which may be full of traps. One of these is to recognize that the opponent's position cannot be invalidated, and to give up opposing it at a certain level, while pointing out at the same time the little importance of that level" (Perelman and Olbrechts-Tyteca 489).

In setting out the conditions for persuasive discourse Perelman and Olbrechts-Tyteca write:

> It is not enough for a man to speak or write; he must also be listened to or read. It is no mean thing to have a person's attention, to have a wide audience, to be allowed to speak under certain circumstances, in certain gatherings, in certain circles. We must not forget that by listening to someone we display a willingness to eventually accept his point of view . . . For argumentation to develop there must be some attention paid to it by those to whom it is directed . . . Under normal circumstances, some quality is necessary in order to speak and be listened to. (17–18)

For Paul to function as an apostle in the Corinthian community he must be able to proclaim his gospel and teach its implications. This he cannot do out of volition alone for he must also evince an *authority* to speak that is recognized by his audience. The Corinthian criticism of Paul's weakness, especially in its concern for the limitations and unreliability of his speech, imperils Paul's authority "to speak and be listened to" and thus threatens to undermine his basic apostolic tasks. The challenge strikes at the heart of his identity as an apostle.

Authority and Power = good section

Authority bears an intimate connection with power. Sociological studies of authority in Paul's communities have stressed this connection while keeping distinct one notion from the other. John Howard Schuetz, in *Paul and the Anatomy of Apostolic Authority*, sees power and authority to be related as source and interpretation:

> Power is the source of authority and authority is a version of power as it interprets power and makes it accessible. Power may be an implicit source . . . or it may be seen as more nearly proximate, or even ultimate. In any event, it is a source, and authority is its interpretation, its application. (21)

In *Paul and Power* Bengt Holmberg's Weberian perspective understands power and authority in terms of the social structures of superiority and subordination. He describes power as the ability of one actor to influence another actor to execute his intentions (8) and authority as a particular ordering of the relationship within which that occurs. For Holmberg, authority does not coerce assent but depends upon the subordinate actor's conviction that to comply with the ruling actor's intention is appropriate. Obedience grows from the subordinate's recognition of authority which, in turn, reflects the power of influence expressed (134–35).[9]

Though different in certain respects, Schuetz and Holmberg share a basic affirmation that authority does not stand on its own capacity. The authority to influence another to act in a particular way or to "speak and be listened to" presupposes power. Authority cannot be exercised apart from its recognition. In confirming authority, however, one recognizes not authority itself, but its underlying power to effect and sustain the action it has called for. Authority expresses the *efficacy* of power and grows from its resources; as *source*, power backs authority and sustains its influence.

The criticism of Paul's weakness, especially in its lurking suspicion that he cannot do what he says, launches an assault on Paul's authority. By challenging the capability of Paul's words and deeds, Corinthian critics seek to expose Paul's lack of power and thereby undermine his authority. In Corinthian eyes weakness expresses powerlessness and implies the absence of a sustaining source to undergird Paul's authority with efficacy and durability. The issue, however, goes beyond the simple fact of efficacy or its absence to a more fundamental point: what constitutes the efficacy of authority and what are the sources of power?

Paul's use of the term *"dynamis"* brings into view certain features of the issue of authority and power.[10] In 1 Corinthians 1–4 *"dynamis"* expresses connotations similar to the sociological notions of authority and power. Frequently juxtaposed with references to *"logos,"* *"dynamis"* suggests the *efficacy* of a word, its capacity to have consequence for those who speak and hear it, and may also point to its divine *backing*. Thus, the word *(logos)* of the cross, though folly to the perishing, enacts the *dynamis* of God which

---

[9] In addition to the studies of Schuetz and Holmberg note also the more recent work of Wayne A. Meeks 111–139.

[10] A methodological point: the sociological concepts "authority" and "power" are theoretical constructions, abstractions whose categories help to understand particular phenomena in Paul's text. Accordingly, "authority" and "power" are metaterms and bear no necessary connection with any given term in Paul's discourse. The consideration of *"dynamis"* is pertinent not because of its common translation as "power" but because it manifests the features of efficacy and durability. On metalanguage, see Barthes 92–93.

destroys the sage's wisdom and thwarts the cleverness of the clever (1:18–19). Similarly, the limitations of Paul's speech *(logos)* yet show spirit and *dynamis* in order that Corinthian faith might be in the *dynamis* of God (2:4–5). In these texts Paul juxtaposes the existence of frail words with their consequential effects. No empty word, Paul's frail speech has authority because it is backed by and articulates God's own *dynamis*.[11]

The evidential character of *"dynamis"* contributes to its function as a backing of authority. Paul's formulaic citation of the marks of an apostle as "signs, wonders, and mighty works *(dynameis)*" (2 Cor. 12:12) shows the potential of the term to signify an empowerment that qualifies one with authority. These marks of an apostle, broadly associated with the signs of pneumatic experience, reflect the nearness of divine presence and the pneumatic's access to it. The pneumatic has authority when others recognize in his or her experience the extraordinary power of God that enables the performance of "signs, wonders, and mighty works." Paul's bringing together "spirit" and *"dynamis"* at 2:4 highlights this evidential character that those features have for the apostle's speech. The evidence for his authority rests on the fact that his speech grows from and points to God's spirit and *dynamis*. In this way, the *dynamis* of God shows itself as both the source of Paul's authority as well as that which is articulated through it.

Paul significantly qualifies God's *dynamis* as being present when he came to Corinth "in weakness and in fear and trembling" (2:3–5; cf. 2 Cor. 12:12). This means that for Paul the presence of God's *dynamis* does not remove the one empowered from the subjecting reach of worldly claims. Here Paul does not dodge the issue of dynamic efficacy—concerned to establish his authority, he can hardly do so—but moves its point of controversy away from the mere fact of *dynamis* to its place in the afflicting world of the apostle. By associating his speech and weakness with *dynamis* Paul claims that what holds true for the pneumatic is no less true for the afflicted apostle: their experience is backed by divine power and thus has the authority to bring others to faith.

Analysis of the diction of *"dynamis"* exposes the deep theological roots of the issue of authority. Where authority requires power,

---

[11] A third text, 4:19–20, juxtaposes *"dynamis"* and speech to suggest that words can be empty, devoid of backing and consequence. The contrast, though, is not between *"dynamis"* and speech as such, but between *"dynamis"* and mere talk.

Paul cannot accept the charge of weakness without at once claiming the sustenance of some source outside his afflicted experience. This he does by pointing to the backing of God's *dynamis* which em-powers his frail speech with efficacy. In doing so he shifts the question away from his powerlessness and to the congruence of that impotency with divine power. Both Paul and the Corinthians likely agree on the fact of Paul's weakness and the understanding of au-thority as emerging from divine power. But therein lies the contro-versy: what constitutes divine power? How does it appear in the world of human affairs? Nesting in the question of authority lurks the theological issue of God's presence in the world. Does the experience of weakness drive away divine presence, signifying the absence of God in the afflicted life? Or does the experience of weakness, as Paul claims, grant a special access to God's presence and the authority it implies?

Weakness and Powerlessness

The perceived criticism of weakness damages Paul's authority most severely if that weakness points to the apostle's powerlessness. Paul himself presupposes that weakness signifies a powerlessness, although he will dispute the implications others draw from that fact. As a form of powerlessness, weakness expresses several connotations that come to bear on the Corinthian controversy.

In the Corinthian letters the *asthen-* word group bears both literal and figurative meanings.[12] Literally, the word group can signify sickness, disease, or other forms of physical disability (e.g., 1 Cor. 11:30) or point more broadly to the general symptoms of limitation, frailty, and finitude that accompany human life in the world (e.g., 1 Cor. 15:43; 2 Cor. 13:4). In the broader range *"astheneia"* marks the domain of human life within which one is subject to the contingencies of existence and thus may include various types of affliction. Figuratively, the word group signifies ignobility and lack of importance (1 Cor. 1:27 and 12:22).

The literal meaning of *"astheneia"* as a physical sickness has particular force in the Corinthian context. In the eyes of a com-

---

[12] Again, the distinction between language *("astheneia")* and metalanguage (powerlessness) should be kept in view (cf. n.10). The diction of *"astheneia"* is pertinent not because one translates it as "weakness" but because it manifests the features of powerlessness.

munity which recognized healing as a sign of the Spirit's presence (1 Cor. 12:9–10, 29–30) the existence of a sick apostle can only suggest the lack of spiritual power. Where Paul claims to have shown the backing of the Spirit in his proclamation (2:4), his affliction suggests the absence of its power manifest in the inability to heal himself. As Jervell has noted, the problem rests not simply with Paul's weakness, but in the combination of his charismatic gifts with that *astheneia* (191–92). That combination riddles the spiritual criteria for authority and insists upon a reinterpretation of power.

Within the broader range of meaning Paul commonly associates *astheneia* and powerlessness.[13] Whether as sickness or some other form of constraint *"astheneia"* signifies a lack of power fully to initiate and sustain a given course of action. In weakness the afflicted person knows finitude and frailty as a vulnerability to "alien power"; in short, as powerlessness. The experience of *astheneia* coincides with the force of those elements in human life over which one has no control.[14] As such, the figurative meaning of *"astheneia"* as "insignificant" fully implies the powerlessness expressed in the literal meaning: where powerlessness is complete one will perceive the weak as insignificant for they retain no power to signify or to act. In this way the plight of weakness becomes double-edged. On the one hand, as an affliction, weakness impairs the development of one's life and is experienced as suffering; on the other, as the resulting powerlessness, it takes away one's ability to overcome suffering and threatens to perpetuate affliction. Weakness endangers authority by robbing one of both the power to act authoritatively and the ability to overcome such impairment.

In 1 Corinthians 1-4 Paul's use of the diction of *"astheneia"*

---

[13] Note the frequent number of times that the *asthen-* word group is interpreted through the language of power, generally designating the human powerlessness which throws into relief the power of God. See 1 Cor. 1:25–27; 2:3; 15:43; 2 Cor. 12:9–10; 13:3–4,9. Cf. *asthen-* in contrast with strength, 1 Cor. 1:25,27; 2 Cor. 10:10.

[14] Note the similar point made by H. Richard Niebuhr: "For it is part of the meaning of suffering that it is that which cuts athwart our purposive movements. It represents the denial from beyond ourselves of our movement toward pleasure; or it is the frustration of our movement toward self-realization or toward the actualization of our potentialities. Because suffering is the exhibition of the presence in our existence of that which is not under our control, or of the intrusion into our self-legislating existence of an activity operating under another law than ours, it cannot be brought adequately within the spheres of teleological and deontological ethics . . ." (1963:60).

emphasizes its meaning of powerlessness and brings into focus certain of its features.[15] First, Paul's use of asthenic language places weakness over against human boasting (1:29) or any attempt to root faith in human wisdom or power (2:5). It calls into question the human pretense to rule or control the transactions of life (4:8). In this discourse weakness bears the freight of an intrinsic powerlessness, for its critical force challenges precisely the human claim to power.

Second, with the language of weakness Paul points broadly to the arena of life in which the weak are subject to various expressions of "alien power". Confined to no particular affliction, weakness includes those things which lack wisdom and significance no less than that which lacks strength.[16] This breadth suggests that even where Paul does not use the *asthen-* word group, but concedes limitation, he may yet invoke the phenomenon of weakness. For instance, two of the asthenic texts (2:1–5 and 4:9–13) occur in the chain of concessions referring back to Paul's Corinthian ministry. Other texts in that pattern (1:13–17; 3:1–4; 4:1–5) may also be understood as concessions of weakness insofar as they admit some dimension of Paul's powerlessness.

Third, the weakness of Paul threatens the recognition of his authority. The assertion of authority always implies some form of boasting that communicates the claimant's power to initiate and sustain a given course of action. Paul's use of weakness does not put an end to boasting or to the significance of power. Its critical force, however, does sever any connection between the assertion of authority and the backing of human power in its own right. Consequently, from the point of view that values the claim of intrinsic human power (cf. 4:8–10), Paul's assertion of authority makes no sense whatsoever. If he is to remain an apostle for the Corinthians Paul *must* answer the Corinthian criticism. Assessed by the canons of human power his claim to authority has no backing and collapses with the admission of weakness. Yet, as we have suggested earlier, every concession may contain a trap. If Paul's confession endangers his authority, it simultaneously calls into question the formulation of power that warrants the indictment against him.

---

[15] The pertinent texts are 1:18–31; 2:1–5; and 4:9–13.
[16] The tight parallelism of the triadic formulations in 1:18–31 and the seeming interchangeability of wisdom and power in 2:1–5 support this breadth.

The Apologetic Motive

To defend oneself against criticism implies the importance of doing so. The criticism of Paul's weakness challenges his authority and thereby urges his apology, but the motives are more concrete. What are the consequences should Paul fail to defend his authority? What depends upon his successful apology?

1 Corinthians 1–4 culminates in the exhortation for the Corinthians to imitate Paul (4:16). This exhortation, introduced by *"parakalō,"* utilizes a formal pattern through which Paul emphasizes his concrete purposes in writing.[17] If by writing he aims to promote his imitation, then the defense of his weakness is crucial. Apart from this defense he has neither the authority to instruct, nor the possibility of convincing his readers. To imitate another means that one attaches some value to the person or behavior being imitated (cf. Perelman and Olbrechts-Tyteca 363). Unvindicated, Paul only offers the mandate to suffer without establishing the value of doing so—a matter which could hardly be self-evident given the extreme portrait of hardship painted in the preceding verses (4:9–13). The persuasiveness of Paul's exhortation and the defense of his authority converge at the issue of weakness. Corinthian imitation of Paul presupposes the authority of his weakness and, at the same time, is its proof.[18]

1 Corinthians 1-4 also prepares the way for the teaching which follows in the remainder of the letter. From chapter seven forward Paul responds to queries made in a letter from the Corinthians. These sections, clearly marked by their repeated introduction *(peri de),* find Paul instructing the Corinthians on sexual relations, marriage, food offered to idols, spiritual gifts, and the collection for the saints (see 7:1, 25; 8:1; 12:1; 16:1,12). The opening discourse, in its defense of Paul's authority, establishes his prerogative to teach. Because his authority is already under fire—the Corinthian questions may themselves imply veiled objections (Hurd 113)—Paul's intention to respond to the letter cannot occur without first rehabilitating his right to be heard.

---

[17] On the *parakalō* periods, see the respective work of Bjerkelund and of Mullins. Note that the discourse of 1 Corinthians 1–4 is framed by *parakalō* periods at its beginning (1:10) and conclusion (4:16), accenting the importance of the form within the letter.

[18] On the centrality of the notion of imitation in Paul, note Patte 1983: 133–39 and 340–47.

A third motive, more implicit than the first two, concerns Paul's proclamation. The Corinthian criticism attests a misunderstanding and rejection of Paul's gospel. When the Corinthians reject Paul's weakness they deny the authority of a crucified Messiah and the power of God to bring forth strength from weakness. A demand motivates Paul's defense that cannot be reduced to an epistolary necessity. Even if Paul were to have no exhortation to give nor instruction to offer he yet would have to defend himself for the rejection of his apostleship declares too loudly the competing convictions of the gospel of human power. The issue of authority decisively effects his future relations with the Corinthian community. But in its depths, the issue exposes the theological ground of Paul's activity. One cannot separate the authority to preach the gospel from the meaning of the gospel itself. As such, Paul's apology is urgent and unavoidable.

THE HOMILETIC CONTEXT

Any rhetorical situation reflects not only the speaker's self-perception but his or her perception of the audience being addressed. Accordingly, the apologetic context, in its focus upon Paul's identity as one under criticism, does not exhaust the rhetorical situation. Another context of argument, the homiletic, also confronts the reader and grants access to Paul's perception of the Corinthians. In 1 Corinthians 1-4, the rhetorical situation compels such a double focus. As apologetic, the rhetorical exigence appears as Paul's need to defend himself; but, within the homiletic perspective, the same exigence appears as the Corinthian need to reinterpret their calling. The exigence is singular, but must be articulated in this complex manner for the success of Paul's defense can only coincide with the Corinthian reinterpretation of their calling. The fulfillment of the one task cannot occur without the other.

Paul's attempt to provoke a reinterpretation of the Corinthian calling constitutes his homiletic aim. As with "apology," we use the term "homily" not in any formal or generic sense (cf. Wuellner and Borgen), but to express a rhetorical focus on the edification of Paul's hearers. In this sense the homiletic dimensions of 1 Corinthians 1–4 spring from the rhetorical situation and the demands of argumentation. We will discuss these dimensions in terms of the interrelationship of the calling of Paul and the Corinthians, the diction of *klēsis*, and the contours of God's call to salvation.

The Interrelationships of Calling

All argumentation presupposes certain shared agreements between a speaker and an audience. Minimally, a common language must exist, even if only to highlight disagreement. To proceed further a speaker must either assume or establish common places of facts and truths, conventions, values, and various hierarchies (Perelman and Olbrechts-Tyteca 65–114). The recognition of common constraints provides a framework through which one can argue and engage in meaningful discourse. In bringing that recognition to the surface, however, the speaker may already be at work to promote his or her cause. By pointing to common assumptions a speaker creates an ethos of kinship that softens the adversity of argument, a sense of communion that allows him or her to say "I am one of you". Moreover, the speaker claims a further rhetorical advantage by binding the audience to the "commonly-held" constraints that he or she chooses to bring into play.

In 1 Corinthians 1–4 Paul establishes a common place through the notion of "calling." From the very outset the proliferation of *kaleō*- cognates in the address (1:1–3) and thanksgiving (1:4–9) insures the prominence of the theme. Paul identifies himself as one "called to be an apostle" (1:1) and proceeds to name the Corinthians as those "called to be saints" (1:2) and "those whom God has called into the fellowship of his son" (1:9). Here Paul does not imply that he and the Corinthians share the same calling, but that the same God has called both to their respective realities in Christ. The resulting kinship allows Paul to speak of God as "*our* father" (1:3) and of Jesus Christ as "*our* Lord" (1:9). In relating himself to the Corinthians as one claimed by the same caller, he enhances his communion with the audience and furnishes a framework for meaningful discourse.

If called to distinct circumstances Paul and the Corinthians yet share a common calling to certain dimensions of worldly life. Early in the discourse Paul encourages a consideration of the Corinthian calling and details its contours through the triad "not many were wise as the world deems wisdom, not many were powerful, and not many were well-born" (1:26). These features Paul then correlates with God's claim upon the foolish, weak, and insignificant things of the world (1:27–28) and later, his own description of apostolic life (4:10). The dimensions of the Corinthian calling and Paul's apostolic life share the domain of powerlessness as the arena of God's claim. In this way Paul forbids his reader to separate the apologetic and homiletic concerns or to dismiss apostolic weakness as an irrelevant concern.

The Diction of Klēsis

Critics disagree over the meaning of "calling" in 1 Corinthians. Centering on the two texts in which Paul uses "klēsis," 1:26 and 7:20, recent exegesis has interpreted the term as either a reference to God's call to salvation (Bartchy) or to the social circumstances in which one is called (Theissen). The two readings need not exclude each other. On the one hand, the Corinthian klēsis (1:26) does not reflect simply a social circumstance, but a sphere of life claimed by God to oppose the human boast (1:29) and thereby effect salvation (1:30). On the other hand, Paul does not use "klēsis" as a free-floating theological metaphor: God's call to salvation is shaped by its concrete implications and issues in an imperative. Anchored to its triadic qualification (1:26), God's call to the Corinthians precludes the human boast through its linking salvation with the concrete features of life that lack intrinsic power. In 1:26–31 God's call to salvation requires seriousness about the circumstances of its reception, for it is those circumstances that God claims to save the Corinthians from the human boast.

In bringing together God's klēsis and the Corinthians' relative absence of wisdom, power, and status, Paul not only qualifies the community as klētoi, but makes a statement about the salvation to which God has called them. The circumstance of the Corinthians is not a precondition for some salvation which follows, but already reflects a salvation that overcomes human boasting (1:29), exists in Christ (1:30), and boasts in the Lord (1:31). As such, the call to salvation does not subsequently overcome the lowly Corinthian plight, but insures it as the perpetual vantage point from which they perceive their salvation. God's call does not lead away from the impoverished circumstances of its enunciation, but calls to salvation precisely in its claim upon those circumstances.

The Contours of God's Call to Salvation

The enunciation of God's calling always occurs within a context of human activity. In 1 Corinthians 1–4 Paul draws the contours of God's call to salvation, bringing into focus a context or a "world" in which that call can be received. As he marks those contours Paul also opposes any attempt to locate the divine calling outside their bounds (which he understands the Corinthians to have done). The Corinthian controversy reflects a dispute over the contours of God's call to salvation: in what context is it experienced, recognized as salvific, and taken as a measure of life? God has called both Paul and the Corinthians, but they stand divided on the implication of that call and the terms of its appropriation.

S. Scott Bartchy has argued that

> Paul and the Corinthians represent two very different ways of apprehending reality, which allowed the same words to carry two different sets of meanings. They had shared the beginning of a common language during Paul's ministry there. A field of language had been laid down on which they could meet each other. But their 'meetings' often seem to have been superficial, most probably because the Corinthians perceived reality in terms which were fundamentally spatial . . . whereas Paul perceived reality in terms which were basically temporal. (174)

The issue of calling provides a case in point of such a "mismeeting." A common point within a field of language, the notion of calling offers a framework within which a meeting can occur, yet itself becomes controversial in the particulars of its appropriation. Within the common place of calling Paul and the Corinthians only appear to meet or to meet superficially for they stand far apart in their perception of the contours of God's calling. As Bartchy noted, this estrangement grows from their "different ways of apprehending reality" (an issue we will pursue at length in the next chapter). The difference, however, does not seem to reflect a Corinthian over-emphasis on the spatial as much as a way of perception that distorts both the temporal and spatial perspectives from which the Corinthians have understood their existence. Paul aims to reorient the Corinthians away from those perspectives and toward that which allows them to recognize the spatial and temporal contours of their calling in the word of the cross.

The Temporal Perspective

Recent interpreters have stressed that Paul opposes a Corinthian enthusiasm which has collapsed the futurity of salvation into the present. In their spiritual and sacramental lives the Corinthians believe themselves already to possess the full gifts of salvation and even now are "living it up in glory" (Robinson 33). According to this line of interpretation Paul shows the prematurity of enthusiasm by

the use of apocalyptic tradition, unleashing on his audience the bite
of his eschatological reservation: *not yet* has the fullness of salvation
become a lived reality.[19] Such a temporal reading stands on firm
ground in its capacity to relate diverse issues throughout the correspondence (Meyer 1965:14) but must be complemented with sensitivity to the spatial question of worldly existence. Corinthian prematurity itself grows from a misunderstanding of salvation that
skews both the "where" and "when" of God's calling (see Plank
1981:50–54 and Doughty).

The temporal indices of 1 Corinthians 1–4 document Paul's
perception of the loss of the futurity of salvation. In these chapters
Paul demarcates both the present and future and seeks to block any
path of flight from the former to the latter. At the outset he sets off
the future from the present as a time of revelation which must be
awaited (1:7), a *telos* until which one must be sustained (1:8). As a
time of disclosure the future makes any present judgment premature (4:5) or claim to wisdom deceptive (3:18). Accordingly, the
otherness of the future clarifies the present as a time of waiting and a
season of need (1:7–8), a time in which darkness hides human
intention (4:5) and true wisdom springs from folly (3:18). The present, as embodied in the life of Paul, remains the hour in which
affliction persists and apostles live in subjection to human plight
(4:9–13). Moreover, it is the moment of God's calling to precisely
those realities. If, in the present, the realities of affliction and
limitation persist, they also come then to be claimed by God for his
own purpose.

Paul's characterization of Corinthian behavior as premature or
untimely indicates that, in his eyes, they have abdicated this present. The imperatives not to pass judgment *before the time* (4:5) and
not to be deceived by a wisdom alien to *this age* (3:18) signify Paul's
perception that judgments were being rendered as if the end had
brought its illumination of hidden things and that self-deception was
obscuring the peculiar criterion of wisdom in the present age.[20]
Further, Paul qualifies such self-deception in a decidedly temporal
way: the Corinthians, at the time of his foundation preaching, were
"not yet" *(oupo)* spiritually mature and were "still now" *(eti nun)* in

---

[19] This line of interpretation is widespread. See, e.g., the respective works of
Kaesemann, Robinson, Wilckens, Meyer (1965), and Plank (1981).
[20] The syntax of Paul's present imperatives presupposes that the prohibited
activities were already in progress. See Blass and Debrunner #336.

their infancy (3:1–2); their claim to satiety and wealth Paul satirizes as premature—"Already *(ēdē)* you are filled! Already you have become rich . . ." (4:8).

In addressing the Corinthians who share with the apostle a call to salvation, Paul confronts the issue of whether or not that call obliterates the constraints of the present and its distinct shaping of salvation. For him, it does not. For his audience, however, it has led to a collapse of present and future which, in Paul's eyes, renders their appropriation of God's call premature and their salvation other than that born in this age of God's folly.

The Spatial Perspective

1 Corinthians 1–4 contains few spatial images. The temporal dimensions of the situation, however, imply a peculiar spatial orientation that describes the Corinthians no less than does their prematurity. Corinthian enthusiasm misunderstands the worldly character of salvation—its roots in powerlessness—and thus perpetuates a world-alienation along with its anachronism. The Corinthians purchase flight from the present at price of this world and its realities.[21]

The prematurity of the Corinthian orientation requires an accompanying world-alienation, for the world's continued expression of weakness and folly sharply distinguishes the present from the future. Persisting in its unredeemed features, the world's current reality gives the lie to any confidence about the present fullness of salvation. Not yet has the present become the awaited future of salvation for, in affliction, the world still cries for redemption. Those who would maintain the conviction that salvation has already occurred must place themselves outside the domain of affliction and thus, outside the world in which it is a salient feature. For Paul, such an otherworldly orientation places the Corinthians not only in a net of deception, but outside the province of God's call to salvation among the weak and foolish things of the world.

In Paul's eyes, the Corinthians flee no uncharted expanse, but a world that has assumed a particular configuration in 1 Corinthians 1–4. Within its bounds one finds not only the various appearances of strength and weakness, but their fundamental opposition. As Paul maps the world of human experience he gives to the region of

---

[21] On the problem of worldliness in 1 Corinthians see Plank 1985 and, more broadly, Meyer 1979–80.

powerlessness the markers of sacred space.[22] Here where persons
know weakness, folly, and disgrace, God issues the call to salvation
and founds the "world" of *koinōnia* with the crucified Messiah (1:9).
Outside, where persons seek strength, wisdom, and honor (4:10),
lies profane space—not a province beyond God's activity, but the
place where God acts to expose existent things as nothing (1:28). As
their criticism of Paul's weakness and their own temporal enthusiasm indicate, the Corinthian orientation can make no peace with the
region of powerlessness and thereby can only misconstrue salvation
as otherworldly or a matter of human power. Their flight from the
world of God's calling, be that through spiritual otherworldliness or
uncompromised affinity for the profane space of human power,
leaves them at odds with the afflicted apostle but no less alienated
from the worldly circumstance of their own call to salvation.

THE RHETORICAL EXIGENCE - N.B.

The apologetic and homiletic contexts of argument show that
Paul seeks to redress a two-fold need through the writing of 1 Corinthians 1–4. As an afflicted apostle he must defend his authority
against charges of weakness that imply a lack of power to sustain his
apostleship; as one whose audience has turned away from the realities of weakness, especially in the appropriation of their own calling, he must bring about a reorientation of the Corinthian sensibility. Closely interrelated, Paul's successful defense depends upon
and coincides with the Corinthian reorientation.

Though discrete in focus, the apologetic and homiletic contexts
merge into a singular exigence. Paul can weave together these
aspects of the discourse because they rest upon the common conviction that, in the cross, God has claimed those things which are
foolish, weak, and ignoble such that they no longer signify only
powerlessness, but the divine power to bring life. The acceptance of
this conviction is the singular exigence of Paul's discourse. To reject
Paul's afflicted apostleship or to flee the bounds of the world's

---

[22] Note Mircea Eliade's description of "sacred space": "When the sacred manifests itself in any hierophany, there is not only a break in the homogeneity of
space; there is also revelation of an absolute reality, opposed to the nonreality of
the vast surrounding expanse. The manifestation of the sacred ontologically
founds the world. In the homogeneous and infinite expanse, in which no point of
reference is possible and hence no orientation can be established, the hierophany reveals an absolute fixed point, a center" (21).

scandal denies God's identification with the weak and attributes to human strength an idolatrous power. But the acceptance of that apostleship and the open embrace of human weakness proclaims clearly Paul's conviction that God has backed the powerless with his power to save.

Convictions bear the freight of systems of value and imply ways of apprehending the world. Paul's conviction, although here cast in the imagery of the cross and human weakness, goes beyond its theological reference to suggest a style of knowing reality. Where God brings strength from weakness the world becomes an icon of paradox to be known only with openness to irony. The way of the cross and the way of irony are one way. Paul leads his readers to discover its trace.

Chapter III

THE RHETORIC OF IRONY IN 1 CORINTHIANS
4:9–13

> Theology should sail into the contest over reality or strike its colors.
>
> ROBERT FUNK
> *Jesus as Precursor*

> As philosophy begins with doubt, so also that life which may be called worthy of a human being begins with irony.
>
> SØREN KIERKEGAARD
> *The Concept of Irony*

Paul confronts the Corinthian situation armed with the weapons of irony. Through the careful use of ironic language he challenges the Corinthian system of value and asserts the force of his own fundamental convictions. As required by the several levels of the rhetorical situation, Paul's irony pervades the discourse: on the textual surface it works to fulfill Paul's apologetic and homiletic demands, while in the deep structures of the text, it promotes the convictional change that enables those demands to be met.

Paul shows a rich and varied use of symbolic language in 1 Corinthians 1–4. No one rhetorical strategy or device, however, is more apt in the Corinthian situation than his use of irony. While irony strikes out at specific objects it never does so simply, for it always communicates something of the nature of reality even when aimed at a well-defined goal. As such, the contours of irony fit well the dimensions of the Corinthian controversy whose precise issues are freighted with conflicting systems of value. Wayne Booth reminds us that irony's earliest observers knew of its reality-bearing capacity:

> From the earliest discussions of irony it has been seen as something that, like metaphor, will not stay graciously in an

assigned position, something that in fact can easily and
quickly expand its own peculiar appeals, move toward domi-
nance, and become some kind of end in itself. From the
beginning, apparently, the word tended to get itself at-
tached to a type of character—Aristophanes' foxy *eirons*,
Plato's disconcerting Socrates—rather than to any one device. The ironist did not simply say something about his
subject, he said something about himself and the world.
(1974:138–139)

In discussing Paul's irony, we concentrate upon 1 Cor.
4:9–13, recognizing it as a focal instance in which Paul's use of irony con-
verges with the apologetic and homiletic demands. Study of this text
provides access to Paul's irony at work and enables us to discern its
rhetorical effect in the discourse at large. Moreover, if 4:9–13 is a
particularly appropriate text for the study of Paul's rhetoric of irony,
the converse is also true: to understand this passage requires a grasp
of Paul's irony.

Our text purports to be a description of Paul and the Corinthians in their respective weakness and strength. However, such a
description only puzzles when read against the discourse as a whole
for while some texts would support this picture, others would appear
to contradict it. We will refer to the former group of texts as the
corroborative texts which include 1:4–9; 2:1–4; and 3:21–22; to the
latter as the *conflicting texts* which include 1:26 and 2:4–7. To
understand 4:9–13 as part of the larger discourse demands reading it
in relation to these corroborating and conflicting texts. The exposure
of Paul's irony enables such a reading.

THE DEFINITION OF IRONY: "GATHERING THE MIST"

The British critic, D. C. Muecke, opens his investigation of
irony with the following disclaimer:

Getting to grips with irony seems to have something in
common with gathering the mist; there is plenty to take
hold of if only one could. To attempt a taxonomy of a
phenomenon so nebulous that it disappears as one approaches is an even more desperate adventure. Yet if, upon
examination, irony becomes less nebulous, as it does, it
remains elusively Protean. (1969:3)

As the critical traditions warn, the broad scope of irony makes it
unlikely that any one definition will be adequate to the phenom-

enon's Protean diversity. The studies of Muecke and Booth clearly show that the workings of irony vary considerably.[1] Any critic who would detect and define its presence must be prepared to confront both diversity of expression and conceptual elusiveness, irony's seductive tendency to flit about or vanish as one draws near with the tools of taxonomy in hand.[2]

The difficulty of defining irony, however, does not mean that it lacks distinguishing features or typically goes unrecognized. On the contrary, in spite of, if not because of its problematic character, readers remain aware of the presence of irony, detecting it through suspicion where definition falls short. As Booth writes, "regardless of how broadly or narrowly he defines irony . . . every reader learns that some statements cannot be understood without rejecting what they seem to say" (1974:1). Though diverse and elusive, irony remains recognizable and describable. For all his shifting shapes and forms Proteus continues to be Proteus and finally submits to Odysseus' inquiry—but only after first interrogating the one who would question him.[3]

Ancient and Modern Definitions of Irony

Both Plato and Aristotle employ the term *eironeia* to describe the self-depreciative mode of behavior of the *eirōn* who, in contrast to the boastful *alazōn*, characteristically understates his capability—generally to critical advantage.[4] With Socrates as a prototype, the *eirōn* takes on the guise of a dissembler, one who toys with the

---

[1] Booth provides a helpful schema of ironic types, classifying them in terms of degree of openness, degree of stability and scope of the "truth revealed" (see 1974:233–35). Muecke's survey of different kinds of irony goes beyond Booth's in comprehensiveness but may be of less actual use due to its complex detail. See *The Compass of Irony* (1969) and also his shorter work, *Irony* (1970).

[2] The elusiveness of irony neither reflects on the skills of the critic nor signifies some inherent flaw in the phenomenon, but is simply a characteristic feature of what is being defined. J. A. Cuddon's comment is to the point: ". . . it seems to be of the essential nature of irony (the need to use the word 'seems' rather than 'it is' is a product of the inherent ambiguousness of the whole concept) that it eludes definition, and this elusiveness is one of the main reasons why it is a source of so much fascinated inquiry and speculation" (1977: s.v. "irony"). Irony introduces an unsettling presence into the terms of any definition including its own.

[3] As with the exchange between Proteus and Odysseus, the critic cannot question irony before first submitting to its force. Cf. Homer, *The Odyssey*, IV:438ff.

[4] See, e.g., Aristotle *EN* 1124b30; 1108a23; *Rhet* 1379b31; and Plato, *Rep* 337a.

appearance of things in order to provoke a reinterpretation of their reality. When brought into the domain of Greek rhetoric, the term continues to express an essential character of dissimulation. It refers to an indirect, if not deceptive, use of language which reflects a difference between what is asserted and what is actually the case.[5]

Although the upending of the *alazōn* gave to the use of irony some positive value, its close tie with deception made it a predominantly pejorative category for the Greeks. Muecke cites several instances of irony's reproachful connotation:

> *"Eironeia"* is first recorded in Plato's *Republic*. Applied to Socrates by one of his victims, it seems to have meant something like "a smooth, low-down way of taking people in". For Demosthenes an *"eiron"* was one who evaded his responsibilities as a citizen by pretending unfitness. For Theophrastus an *"eiron"* was evasive and non-committal, concealing his enmities, pretending friendship, misrepresenting his acts, never giving a straight answer. (1970:14)

As irony passes into the Roman rhetorical tradition, however, its connotation becomes more complimentary, even though the root meaning of dissimulation remains intact. With Cicero and Quintilian the scope of irony broadens from being a rhetorical figure to a manner of discourse itself which could be seen in a more positive light. Thus Quintilian writes that irony could express the ethos "which is commended to our approval by goodness more than aught else and is not merely calm and mild, but in most cases ingratiating and courteous . . ."[6]

Modern theorists have tended to construct their definitions on the legacy of antiquity, treating irony with breadth and retaining a root sense of dissimulation.[7] Definitions of verbal irony have especially appropriated the sense of dissimulation, understanding

---

[5] Commonly such irony was used to blame by ironical praise or to praise by ironical blame. The early overtones of dissimulation and deception become easily absorbed into the rhetorical strategy of saying one thing and meaning the contrary. On the Greek tradition of irony, see N. Knox 3–7; Muecke 1970:14–15; also Abrams, s.v. "Irony".

[6] *Institutio*, VI.ii.9–16; on the breadth of irony see *Institutio*, IX.ii.44–53 and Cicero, *De officiis*, I.30. For a general treatment of the Roman use of irony, see M. LeGuern 47–60.

[7] The breadth of irony was insured by the advances of the Romantic theorists (e.g., A. W. Schlegel, F. Schlegel, and Karl Solger) who insisted that true irony began with contemplation of the world. Accordingly, its breadth was as wide as reality itself and suggested the features of a "cosmic irony."

such irony to involve an intentional linguistic dissimulation that expresses a contrast between the literal meaning of what is stated and the meaning that is implied by a speaker or writer. Thus, Northrop Frye defines irony as a "pattern of words that turns away from direct statement or its own obvious meaning" (40). Abrams defines irony similarly as

> a statement in which the implicit meaning intended by the speaker differs from that which he ostensibly asserts. Such an ironic statement usually involves the explicit expression of one attitude or evaluation, but with the implication of a very different attitude or evaluation (s.v. "Irony").

In modern definition, then, irony reflects "the existence of a second perspective on a statement or action, of which the reader is made aware. This would encompass the statement of an opposite, which the reader can see through, as well as various shades of overstatement and understatement" (Liberman and Foster: s.v. "Irony").

We should note several recurring features of these definitions. First, irony occurs through an *indirect use of language* and expresses a covert meaning. The meaning of ironic language lacks self-evidence and must be reconstructed by the reader. Second, the indirect use of language reflects a *contrast between appearance and reality*. In the ironic text things are not simply as they appear to be. Third, irony works through the *introduction or implication of a second perspective* from which the text's "obvious meaning" can be reinterpreted.[8] Although acute forms of irony may threaten to cast a text into absurdity, irony typically functions not to undermine a text's meaningfulness, but to give access to it by indicating the vantage point from which the text's full meaning can be perceived.

The ironic, second perspective—the very heart of irony's effectiveness—functions similarly to what Peter Berger has described as the "experience of alternation." Alternation occurs when one's world-view and sense of social reality are glimpsed in their artificial character thus becoming subject to criticism and change. In discussing the alternation between world-views and the precariousness which issues from it, Berger quotes an insightful parallel taken from Arthur Koestler's *Arrival and Departure:*

8 Cf. the claim of R. Scholes and R. Kellogg that irony is "the result of a disparity of understanding" made inevitable (in narrative) by the existence of different points of view. The creation of points of view in a narrative bears a marked functional resemblance to the introduction of an ironic, second perspective in a text (see 240–41).

> As children we used to be given a curious kind of puzzle to
> play with. It was a paper with a tangle of very thin blue and
> red lines. If you just looked at it you couldn't make out
> anything. But if you covered it with a piece of transparent
> red tissue-paper, the red lines of the drawing disappeared
> and the blue lines formed a picture—it was a clown in a
> circus holding a hoop and a little dog jumping through it.
> And if you covered the same drawing with a blue tissue-
> paper, a roaring lion appeared chasing the clown across the
> ring. You can do the same thing with every mortal, living or
> dead. You can look at him through Sonia's tissue-paper and
> write a biography of Napoleon in terms of his pituitary gland
> as has been done: the fact that he incidentally conquered
> Europe will appear as a mere symptom of the activities of
> those two tiny lobes, the size of a pea. You can explain the
> message of the Prophets as epileptical foam and the Sistine
> Madonna as the projection of an incestuous dream. The
> method is correct and the picture in itself complete. But
> beware of the arrogant error of believing that it is the only
> one. The picture you get through the blue tissue-paper will
> be no less true and complete. The clown and the lion are
> both there, interwoven in the same pattern. (17–18)

The second perspective of irony functions similarly to Koestler's
tissue-paper. When placed over a text, irony's second perspective
alters the picture one has of that text so that once hidden features of
its meaning come surprisingly into view. The obvious, literal meaning of a statement remains a latent possibility of the text, but irony
forbids the reader to approach it with certainty ("the arrogant error")
as if it were the only meaning possible. Irony reminds the reader
that "the clown and the lion are both there." In becoming aware of
an ironic perspective, readers undergo Berger's "alternation." Neither their first interpretation nor their style of reading can rest
secure before the overlay of irony. With irony, all reading becomes a
matter of "precarious vision."

Still, not all second perspectives are alike anymore than all
tissue-paper is blue. The transparencies of irony vary in texture and
depend upon different mechanisms to set their "alternation" in
motion. In the context of our study two of these ironic perspectives
have special pertinence: the *irony of dissimulation* and the *irony of
paradox*. Their importance to the interpretation of 1 Cor. 4:9–13
warrants detailed discussion of their features.

The Irony of Dissimulation

Both ancient and modern theorists of irony have tended to focus
upon the notion of dissimulation. Such a focus shapes the definition

of irony as a technique by which something *appears* to be other than it really is, a concealment of true identity under some pretense or disguise. In this vein, the *eirōn* of Greek comedy portrays a character who typically understates his capacities by deliberately pretending to be less intelligent than he really is. The enduring image of Socrates' self-depreciation becomes the prototype of dissimulative irony, exemplified in his assumed posture of hoping to learn, for instance, the meaning of justice from the very interlocutor he intends to instruct in the matter.

Two prominent features characterize the irony of dissimulation. First, dissimulative irony depends upon the figures of exaggeration, overstatement and understatement, to set its effect into motion. Dissimulation makes a given feature of a person or situation seem greater or lesser than its actual reality. This exaggeration, however, becomes ironic only with a certain "twist" or polar inversion. Unlike the exaggeration of caricature, dissimulative irony creates a diminished portrayal of great features and an augmented expression of features whose reality is small. The irony of dissimulation transforms the apparent into the implication of its opposite or contrary.

The second feature of dissimulative irony is its use of pretense. In his dissimulation the *eirōn* only disguises his capability, feigning a posture of ignorance so as to disarm the boastful *alazōn*. So, too, from this perspective, Socrates' self-depreciation is a ruse which conceals the actual advantage he holds over his interlocutor. As such, dissimulative irony involves deception and depends upon it to be effective. From the reader's point of view, however, that ironic effect is *not* deception, but a new perception of what is actually the case. The *eirōn*'s dissimulation moves toward reality by unmasking the pretense of the *alazōn*. As readers detect the intended exaggeration in the one case, irony leads them to look for similar exaggeration elsewhere. Dissimulative irony inspires suspicion of the apparent: the accented exaggeration of the *eirōn*'s features points to and unmasks the pretense of the *alazōn*. Ironic dissimulation deceives, but not in bad faith. To the reader, the ironist's lie only reveals truth, enabling a new perception of reality. Ironic exaggeration shows itself to be so and thereby alerts its observers to the lurking presence of pretense.

The Irony of Paradox
       Like the irony of dissimulation, paradoxical irony brings together the expression of one meaning with the communication of its opposite. However, in paradoxical irony the expressed meaning

retains an integrity that differs sharply from the pretense of dissimulation. Where the irony of dissimulation suggests that the expressed meaning appears to be other than it is, the irony of paradox
notes that the expressed meaning *is* what it appears to be, but what
it appears to be is not all that it is. Thus, in this perspective,
Socrates' ignorance is not a clever disguise, but the real awareness of
not knowing which expresses at once the only genuine knowledge.
The true appearance of Socrates as unwise portrays his true wisdom.

Three prominent features characterize paradoxical irony. First,
as the name indicates, such irony depends upon paradox as its
essential mechanism. As William Lynch has defined it, paradox
involves "the unexpected coexistence, to the point of identity, of
certain contraries" (84). Accordingly, the meaning of a text shaped
by paradoxical irony is *both* what it appears to be *and*, at the same
time, precisely the opposite of what it appears to be. Paradox differs
from dissimulation in which contraries do not actually coexist but
merely disguise each other; so, too, does it differ from simple
contradiction in which contraries do coexist but not with identity.
Paradoxical irony encourages the reader to perceive that contraries
do coexist in "a single act of the imagination" (unlike dissimulation)
and that their coexistence is not a mistake (as is the case with
contradiction) (Lynch:83).

Second, paradoxical irony requires the integrity of both the
expressed, apparent meaning of a text and of its opposite value.
Whereas the exposure of dissimulation obviates the meaning of
appearance, paradoxical irony calls for a relative seriousness about
the apparent that refuses to dissolve its significance. Paradoxical
irony can work only through the identity of opposites whose contrariety is given full due and expression. Within the constraints of
paradoxical irony the defender of Socrates' knowledge must take
seriously the philosopher's genuine ignorance for to undermine his
perplexity would only sacrifice the very knowledge to be affirmed.

The third feature of paradoxical irony, closely related to the
second, underscores the *relative* seriousness of paradoxical contraries. Although each contrary term requires full expression, the
paradoxical coupling of contraries denies either term autonomous
meaning. Instead, it points to a perpetual and mutual qualification
of both terms of the paradox. Such qualification relativizes the claim
of either term and disperses the force of any given element. Thus,
for instance, Socrates' paradoxical knowledge, though never less
than knowledge, is also never pristine. Born of perplexity, it has no

life when severed from the ignorance which qualifies it and of which
it is ever aware.

The mutual qualification of paradoxical terms functions in a
double-edged way: if, on the one hand, a paradox relativizes the
meaning of any given term by the presence of its contrary, on the
other hand, it *enlarges* that meaning and opens up a broader horizon
for its interpretation. When read through the "both-and" syntax of
paradox, irony is expansive and not subtractive.[9] The paradoxical
coexistence of ignorance and knowledge relativizes their meanings,
but also gives to each a larger scope than it would have had independently. Ignorance is not simply itself, but also something more,
knowledge. Within paradox, its bounds expand to include the contrary.

Through the mutual qualification of contraries, paradox introduces an instability into irony that further distinguishes it from
dissimulation and freights its expression with a deeper irony of
reality. Dissimulative irony presupposes a well-ordered, stable view
of reality. In looking at Socrates from its perspective, the observers
confront no confusion over the categories "ignorance" and "knowledge." What lacks clarity is simply under which category they
should place Socrates (or his antagonist). In contrast, the irony of
paradox riddles the observers' perceptions of reality so that even the
categories of "ignorance" and "knowledge" lose their self-evidence.
Paradoxical irony blurs the boundaries which distinctly separate the
basic categories of interpretation, boundaries which otherwise
would give to the perception of reality a certain stability and clarity.
The irony of paradox concerns itself less with Socrates than with the
reality of his world.

As a second perspective paradoxical irony inserts between
reader and text a lens which blurs the sharp focus of the text's
meaning. Through this lens the contours of what a reader perceives
takes on a fluid character such that any given textual feature potentially expresses both itself and its contrary. The blurred focus, itself
ironic, ultimately serves not confusion but clarity: paradoxical irony
blurs not what is actually the case, but the semblance, the seeming
stability of the appearance of all things. It risks confusion to make
perception clear.

Through its seeming confusion, paradoxical irony generates in

---

[9] Here I disagree with Booth's claim that "irony is essentially 'subtractive'"
(1974:177).

the reader a suspicion of the literal and the apparent and occasions a reinterpretation of the text's meaning. To this extent, its reader-effect resembles that of dissimulative irony. These effects do, however, differ in the nature of the reinterpretation they provoke. Dissimulative irony allows the reader to reconstruct a stable world of meaning in the reading of the text. Having detected dissimulation, the reader knows that things are not what they appear to be, but remains confident that the irony yet unmasks a reliable order. The categories through which the reader reconstructs the textual world continue to possess a straightforwardness. Only the particular items aligned with those categories undergo the reader's reevaluation.

By contrast, paradoxical irony threatens any attempt of the reader to secure a world of meaning from the text. Here reality itself feels the blows of irony. At a deep level of the paradoxical text, the very categories through which the reader would reconstruct the textual world have become unstable and provide no firm foundation for interpretation. *The reality which paradoxical irony discloses is yet ironic*. The paradoxical text does project a world of meaning, but only constructs it in quicksand. Its most profound effect occurs when the readers realize that they, too, have been caught in its trap and in their reading must remain tentative before the open and enlarged horizon of the ironic text.

Excursus: Kierkegaard and the Ironic

Although we have made no explicit reference to Kierkegaard, the influence of his 1841 dissertation, *The Concept of Irony, With Constant Reference to Socrates*, pervades our discussion. Kierkegaard's sense of the ironic and our paradoxical perspective intersect in at least two ways.

First, although Kierkegaard was well aware of the association of irony with dissemblance, he refused to let that notion define the workings of irony. Indeed, he includes dissemblance in a series of concepts thought to resemble irony significantly, but whose similarity is only proximate. Ultimately, irony differs from dissemblance, even as it does from hypocrisy, satire, doubt, and religious devotion (272-275). Kierkegaard does not, however, pursue this difference in terms of mechanism—for instance, the difference between paradox and exaggeration—but in terms of purpose: "dissemblance . . . has a purpose, an external purpose foreign to dissemblance itself. Irony, on the other hand, has no purpose, its purpose is immanent in itself, a metaphysical purpose. The purpose is none other than irony itself" (272).

Significantly, Kierkegaard pushes irony beyond the bounds of dissimulation. Unlike Kierkegaard, we have argued that dissimulative irony is genuinely an irony—it encourages a perception of the real—but with him we have maintained that irony involves much more than dissimulation. The self-purposive dimensions of irony to which Kierkegaard points illumine a central aspect of paradoxical irony, namely its fundamental character as an irony of reality.[10] As Kierkegaard saw, one undertook dissimulation not simply for the sake of pretense, but for purposes extrinsic to it. Paradoxical irony, however, is less an activity which the ironist undertakes than a feature of reality that he or she discovers. Such a discovery may have particular consequences, but the irony has no purpose as such. The irony of paradox grows not from the ironist's intention to achieve a certain end as much as from his or her observation of the world and the nature of its reality.[11]

Second, Kierkegaard's writing emphasizes the seriousness with which contrary, ironic terms should be taken. In his dissertation he directly confronts this issue in terms of Socrates' ignorance. Here, on the one hand, he distances himself from the view of irony as dissimulation, a view which would make of Socrates' ignorance "merely . . . a form of conversation" (286). On the other hand, he deliberately repudiates a particular expression of this view in the Hegelian suggestion that Socrates was in earnest about his ignorance, but for that reason not ironic.[12] With his characteristic dialectic, Kierkegaard claims instead that Socrates' irony requires that "his ignorance is both to be taken seriously and not to be taken seriously" (286). The same would be true of his knowledge.

[10] The following statement adequately represents Kierkegaard's view: "Irony in the eminent sense directs itself not against this or that particular existence but against the whole given actuality of a certain time and situation. It has, therefore, an apriority in itself, and it is not by successively destroying one segment of actuality after the other that it arrives at its total view, but by virtue of this that it destroys in the particular. It is not this or that phenomenon but the totality of existence which it considers *sub specie ironiae*" (271).

[11] See Muecke's use of a similar contrast to distinguish Verbal and Situational Irony. The former is reckoned from the ironist's point of view ("He is being ironical"); the latter, from the point of view of the ironic observer ("Isn't that ironic?") (1970: 49–51).

[12] This is but an instance of Kierkegaard's larger criticism of Hegel's inconstant argument: Hegel does not permit the view of irony as "infinite absolute negativity" to achieve its full force. Hegel's Socrates does not remain "infinitely negative" and thereby his ignorance is but a passing moment, itself overcome in synthesis. See Mark Taylor 94–99.

At this point Kierkegaard has shaped his view of irony in a distinctly paradoxical way. Socrates' ironic knowledge has no positive content. Keenly aware of the absence of knowledge, he knows "nothing." To take this "nothingness" with absolute seriousness would threaten despair and promote endless quests to arrive at "something"; to attribute to it no seriousness would only foster an illusion. Kierkegaard's way of irony suggests a different response. In his own terms, "Irony is the infinitely delicate play with nothingness, a playing which is not terrified by it but still pokes its head into the air" (286–287). Irony, then, affirms the real existence of "nothingness" but manifests a playful freedom in its midst. Irony strips "nothingness" of its terror by pointing to the simultaneous presence of the knowledge which is the awareness of ignorance.

Accordingly, the terms of irony warrant real, but not absolute seriousness.[13] The ironic coupling of Socrates' ignorance and knowledge transcends the seriousness which either term might command on its own. "Knowledge" and "ignorance" do not become something *other* than they were (such that we would not take them seriously), but something *more*. Kierkegaard's irony summons seriousness, but requires the tentativeness of one prepared to witness the playful batting of all meaning into the air.

THE DETECTION OF IRONY

Though forceful, irony works in subtle ways. To detect its presence in a literary text requires sensitivity to context and a certain judgment as to the author's convictions and intentions. As Booth has argued, an ironic text will manifest certain clues or hints that expose its irony, or at least make the reader suspicious of its obvious, literal meaning. To detect irony, he directs the reader to consider the following types of clues: straightforward warnings in the author's own voice (e.g., titles, epigraphs); open proclamation of error (e.g.,

[13] Kierkegaard provides an apt example: ". . . The same is true with Socrates' ignorance: it is the nothingness whereby he destroys every knowledge. This can best be seen from his conception of death. He is ignorant of what death is and what is after death, whether there be something or nothing at all, completely ignorant. But he does not take this ignorance any further to heart; on the contrary, he feels quite properly free in this ignorance. He is not serious about this ignorance, and yet he is dead serious about the fact that he is ignorant" (287).

violation of popular expression, historical fact, or conventional judgment); conflicts of fact within the work; clashes of style; and conflicts of belief (i.e., between the beliefs expressed and the beliefs we suspect the author to hold) (1974:55–73 and 1978:7–9).

Paul's description in 4:9–13 and its literary context give evidence of a number of these indices of irony. First, although the text shows relatively few straightforward warnings of Paul's irony, its context does provide a clear instance at 4:8. Following an increasingly climactic sequence of statements that first appear to praise the Corinthians, Paul appends a qualification that takes back the final claim just made. He addresses the Corinthians,

> Already you are sated, already you have become rich, apart from us you have become kings.

But then he adds,

> I wish that indeed you had become kings *(kai ophelon ge ebasileusate)*, in order that we might share your kingly power.

Paul's wishing for what he seemingly had just claimed to be true alerts the reader to his indirection, a clue further accented by the unattainability of the wish.[14] Standing over against the apostle's previous statement the wish suggests a non-literal meaning. It implies a second perspective through which the readers should understand his "praise" of the Corinthians.

Second, the context which directly frames 4:9–13 provides another warning that Paul does not mean literally what he says. The apostle establishes a climate of criticism in 4:7 ("why do you boast. . .?") which he extends in 4:14 ("Not to shame you do I write these things, but to warn you . . ."). If Paul means simply to praise the Corinthians then he has obscured the connection between such praise and the boasting he opposes (4:7) and how such praise risks shame and begets warning (4:14). Again the text invites the reader to be suspicious of the literal meaning of Paul's claims in these verses.

Third, a number of ambiguities, if not conflicts of fact and belief, exist in the relationship between 4:9–13 and the rest of chapters 1–4. The material which precedes 4:9–13 anticipates much of the con-

---

[14] With the imperfect or aorist indicative, *ophelon* is used in Hellenistic Greek to express an unattainable wish. See Blass and Debrunner #359.

ceptuality of the description of affliction, a feature that prepares
Paul's readers to hear these verses in a particular way. However, in
that material Paul has offered comments about himself and the
Corinthians that in certain instances support the literal sense of 4:9–
13 (the corroborative texts) whereas in other instances they only
conflict with it (the conflicting texts).

Both 4:8 and 4:10 attest Paul's ambiguity and the possibility of
irony. In 4:8 the initial description of the Corinthians as sated
(*kekoresmenoi*), rich (*eploutēsate*), and having royal power (*ebasileu-
sate*) receives some support in the letter's thanksgiving. There Paul
notes that they do not lack for any spiritual gift (1:7) and are "enriched in every way" (*en panti eploutisthēte;* 1:5).[15] At the same
time, however, Paul describes the Corinthians who are "filled" as
also not yet ready to partake of "solid food" (3:2); he notes that the
same rich ones have nothing that has not been given them (4:7) and
wishes those with royal power the possibility of reigning (4:8). His
description of the Corinthians in 4:8 finds a parallel in his twice-
made affirmation, "all things are yours" (*panta humōn;* 3:21–22).
However, as he qualifies that affirmation—"but you are Christ's"
(*humeis de Christou;* 3:23)—so does he temper the description of
Corinthian strength by a counter-picture of their inadequacy.

The antithetical attributions of 4:10 show a similar complexity.
Here Paul contrasts himself as an apostle with the Corinthians:
where he is a fool (*mōroi*), they are wise (*phronimoi*); where he is
weak (*astheneis*), they are strong (*ischuroi*); and where his reputa-
tion is tarnished (*atimoi*), they are held in honor (*endoxoi*). Paul's
self-description receives support not only from the afflictions to
which he calls attention in 4:11–12, but from other acknowledg-
ments made earlier in the discourse: a fool, his proclamation lacks
words of wisdom (2:1–4); a person of weakness, Paul approaches the
community in weakness (*en astheneiai;* 2:3) and with much fear and
trembling (*en phobō kai en tromō pollō;* 2:3); one in disrepute, he is
subject to community judgment (4:3), championed by one group but
opposed by others (1:12), and perceived to be untrustworthy in his
travel plans (4:18). The same Paul, however, does claim to impart

---

[15] The *plouteō* cognates (1:5 and 4:8) are easily correlated. Although less direct,
another correlation exists between the Corinthians' satiety (4:8) and their not
lacking in any spiritual gift (1:7). The verb *korennumi* (4:8) commonly refers to
being filled with food, but also has the figurative meaning of having everything
that one needs. Note, too, that food imagery is often conjoined with discussion
of spiritual nourishment (e.g., 3:1–2), thus securing the correlation further.

wisdom (*sophia;* 2:6–7) and demonstrate power (*dynamis;* 2:4); further, he also parades before the Corinthians his "honorable" credentials as one called by the will of God to be an apostle (1:1), commissioned by God (3:10), a co-worker of God (3:9), and the founder of the Corinthian church, their father (4:15).

The attributions of the Corinthians continue in the direction of 4:8, but bear an even closer "mirrored" relation to 1:26–28, as do Paul's own attributes. In 1:26–28 Paul first describes the Corinthian calling as one in which few were wise (*sophoi*), powerful (*dynatoi*) or well-born (*eugeneis*); he then proceeds through careful synonymity and opposition to detail God's paradoxical reversal of these very categories. Thus, where few Corinthians were wise (*sophoi*), Paul portrays God as the one who claims the foolish things of the world (*ta mōra tou kosmou*) in order to put the wise things (*tous sophous*) to shame; where few were powerful (*dynatoi*), God claims the weak things of the world (*ta asthenē tou kosmou*) to put to shame the strong (*ta ischura*); and where few were well-born (*eugeneis*) God claims what is not well-born (*agenē*), even despised things (*ta exouthenēmena*), things that have no existence (*ta mē onta*), to shame those things which do (*ta onta*). The following chart displays the relationships between 4:10 and 1:26–28.

Paul (4:10)	Corinthians (4:10)	Corinthians (1:26)	God's Claim (1:27–28)	God's Nullification (1:27–28)
moroi	phronimoi	ou polloi sophoi	ta mōra	tous sophous
astheneis	ischuroi	ou polloi dynatoi	ta asthenē	ta ischura
atimoi	endoxoi *but ἐν Χριστῷ*	ou polloi eugeneis	agenē ta exouthen– ēmena ta mē onta	ta onta

The description of the Corinthians in 1:26 provides a marked contrast with their characterization in 4:10; in fact, the Corinthians of 1:26 are virtually identical with Paul, their antithetical complement in 4:10 and conversely, the Corinthians of 4:10 embody the realities that God has nullified in 1:27–28. Thus Paul's reader finds in 4:10 an even stronger sense of conflicting description than in 4:8, a clashing of perspectives that can only set the stage for an ironic reading.

In both 4:8 and 4:10 Paul's readers find echoes of other portions of chapters 1–4. To the extent that the parallel material conflicts with those descriptions the reader can be suspicious of their literal claim and on the alert for irony. At the same time, the corroborative parallels should not be ignored for they suggest enough possibility to the literal meaning that any irony becomes subtly enhanced by its uncertainty.

Paul's style provides the fourth and final source for the detection of irony. The number of literary and rhetorical devices employed in these verses—antithesis, parallelism, metaphor, repetition—show that Paul here uses a style set apart from direct communication. The abundance of Paul's symbolic speech leads his reader to anticipate the various strategies of indirect communication including irony.

THE IRONIC PERSPECTIVES OF 4:9–13

Both the irony of dissimulation and the irony of paradox interact in 4:9–13. The dissimulative irony, in this context, has a limited function, reflecting elements of exaggeration and inversion in Paul's description. However, the more open-ended and fundamental irony of paradox strikes at the interpretation of that description. In this perspective, the irony focuses not on Paul and the Corinthians as such, but pervades the categories by which they are described.

The Irony of Dissimulation in 4:9–13

Paul utilizes dissimulative irony at 4:9–13 to provoke his readers' reinterpretation of themselves and their apostle. The exaggeration necessary for such irony requires the appropriation of two vantage points, that of the corroborative texts (1:4–9; 2:1–4; 3:21–22) and that of the conflicting texts (1:26 and 2:4–7). When seen against the backdrop of the corroborative texts—texts which support the picture of Paul's weakness and the Corinthian's strength—the exaggeration appears to be simple overstatement, heightening the contrast between the apostle and the Corinthians. For instance, the picture of the Corinthians as sated, wealthy monarchs (4:8) exceeds the more reserved claims of the corroborative texts: although they lack no spiritual gift, the Corinthians must yet wait for the revelation of the lord (1:7); although all things are theirs, they yet are Christ's (3:21–23). This picture exaggerates the Corinthian strength by ignoring the qualifications that had framed their depiction in the corroborative texts.

Similarly, the portrayal of Paul as "the world's refuse" and "the offscouring of all things" (4:13) goes beyond the earlier claim that the apostle was present with much fear and trembling (2:3). The "weakness" of 2:1–4 assumes cosmic dimensions in 4:9–13 as Paul progresses from being the Corinthians' fool to existing as a spectacle before the world, angels, and the human community (4:9). Where earlier Paul referred to his weakness, he now writes of the more sober fate of one living under a death writ (4:9). The "untwisted" overstatement emphasizes the extreme character of the portrayal of Paul's weakness and Corinthian strength. Here the exaggeration conserves rather than inverts those features, giving them strong accent while doing so.

However, from the vantage point of the conflicting texts—texts which oppose the picture drawn in 4:9–13—the reader confronts a different situation. From this perspective the text appears as an inversion of Paul's earlier descriptions: he describes the Corinthians, the majority of whom reflect a calling that brands them as neither wise, powerful, nor well-born (1:26), in terms that exaggerate their significance to the other extreme—they are prudent, strong, and honored (4:10);[16] he portrays himself, one who imparts wisdom (2:6) and manifests spirit and power (2:4), in terms that understate his significance to the other extreme—he is foolish, weak, and in disrepute (4:10). The twisted exaggeration calls into question the apparent claim of 4:9–13 and suggests that in this text things may not be what they seem to be.

Characteristically, dissimulative irony works to allow the reader to unmask pretense. The inverted exaggeration of 4:9–13 functions in precisely that way. Once detected by the readers, the inverted exaggeration of the apostle's self-description leads them to look for similar inversion elsewhere. In this case, the text leads the Corinthian readers to reexamine their own self-perception in order to respond to their portrayal. Perceiving the inverted exaggeration in Paul's case and recognizing the tight, antithetical parallelism of 4:10, no reader can avoid calling into question the depiction of the Corinthians. The reader may reject the validity of Paul's portrayal, but does not have the luxury of ignoring its provocation, the question it raises concerning the Corinthian identity. Unmistakably, Paul's own

[16] The depiction in 4:10 reflects Paul's perception of the Corinthian self-perception. The force of 4:8 and the broader apologetic context would require such a reading. On the relation of 1:26 and 4:10 see Theissen: 233–35.

dissimulation points an accusing finger at the pretense of Corinthian power.

Above all, dissimulative irony works to call into question the literal dimensions of a text. From the vantage point of the conflicting texts Paul's language does not function as straightforward description. Neither does it function in this way when read from the perspective of the corroborative texts. In neither case does Paul literally mean what he says. Still, the force of the corroborative texts acts to conserve a literal claim in "what he says." To say that Paul does not literally mean his self-description as "the offscouring of all things" does not imply that he does not mean what he says in describing himself as an afflicted apostle. The text presupposes a literal claim of the apparent and conserves its force in exaggeration. The claim of Paul's weakness or the Corinthians' strength survives its exaggeration to be communicated all the more powerfully in over-statement. This claim also survives the counter-movement of inversion and remains recognizable in the tension between 4:9–13 and the conflicting texts. If the tension between these perspectives suggests that "things may *not* be what they seem to be" it also communicates some sense of how "things *do* seem to be."

The discourse requires the vantage points of both the corroborative and conflicting texts. Their presence does not indicate simple confusion on Paul's part. Neither group of texts provides a norm that governs the discourse as a whole and against which description might be measured. Rather, they interact to present a view of Paul and the Corinthians greater than what either perspective, when taken singly, might afford. The description occurs through this interaction and comes to expression *between* them.

Recent work done in the phenomenology of reading by Wolf-gang Iser provides a conceptuality to understand this interaction (1978:96–103). Iser would understand the double vantage points to constitute the horizon of Paul's discourse against which the text expresses given themes. He writes,

> As perspectives are continually interweaving and interact-ing, it is not possible for the reader to embrace all perspec-tives at once, and so the view he is involved with at one particular moment is what constitutes for him the 'theme'. This, however, always stands before the 'horizon' of the other perspective segments in which he had previously been situated . . . Now the horizon is not a purely optional one; it is made up of all those segments which had supplied the themes of previous phases of reading. For instance, if

the reader is at present concerned with the conduct of the hero—which is therefore the theme of the moment—his attitude will be conditioned by the horizon of past attitudes toward the hero. . . . The continual interaction of perspectives throws new light on all positions linguistically manifested in the text, for each position is set in a fresh context, with the result that the reader's attention is drawn to aspects hitherto not apparent. Thus the structure of theme and horizon transform every perspective segment of the text into a two-way glass, in the sense that each segment appears against the others and is therefore not only itself but also a reflection and illuminator of those others. Each individual position is thus expanded and changed by its relation to the others, for we view it from all the perspectives that constitute the horizon. (1978: 97–98)

In confronting Paul's description at 4:9–13—the "theme of the moment"—the readers are influenced by their previous phases of reading, notably their encounter with the corroborative and conflicting texts.[17] Accordingly, the readers do not read the text pristinely but over against a broader horizon whose conflicting themes make them suspicious of Paul's straightforwardness and whose corroborating themes compel their seriousness about what he has written. The interaction of these themes illumines aspects of Paul's description that would go unnoticed if read in isolation from either segment. Apart from the conflicting texts Paul's exaggeration lacks any ironic twist and loses connection with the implied second perspective that grounds the readers' suspicion of the literal claim; without the corroborative texts the irony lacks subtlety and threatens to devolve into either simple contradiction or a linguistic docetism.

The interaction of conflicting and corroborating themes in Paul's dissimulative irony prevents the readers from abandoning the literal claim of 4:9–13 to a sea of contradiction; but, at the same time, it refuses permission to grant autonomy to the literal claim such that it alone defines "the way things are." As we will show in the next section, the interaction of 4:9–13 with both groups of texts further participates in a more fundamental irony.

The Irony of Paradox in 4:9–13

The second level of irony, the irony of paradox, involves the *meaning* of Paul's description. Distinct from the exaggeration of

[17] Note the similarity to Perelman and Olbrechts-Tyteca (490–491). Iser's horizon perspective, however, implies not only that the earlier phases influence the perception of the latter, but that the latter influences the recollection of the earlier.

dissimulative irony, the irony of paradox occurs through Paul's transvaluation of the terms of his description. With this irony Paul takes
seriously the reality of his weakness, but suggests, through the
introduction of a paradoxical perspective, that the categories of
"strength" and "weakness" are themselves subject to reinterpretation. The paradoxical irony does not intend to say that Paul is not
really weak, but that the value of real strength occurs precisely in his
weakness; not that the Corinthians lack strength, but that their
strength expresses the value of weakness.

Corroboration and Conflict: The Textual Blank

The interacting perspectives of the description prepare the
reader for the deeper, paradoxical irony. As we have suggested, the
literal claim of the corroborative texts insures the "full-bodied"
character of paradoxical irony. These texts reenforce the integrity of
the paradoxical affirmation: the irony of paradox surpasses the deception of strength masquerading as weakness to state more radi-
cally that strength, understood in its full integrity, *is* weakness and
that weakness, in its genuine dimensions, *is* strength. At the outset,
the corroborative texts deny the reader any explanation of 4:9–13
that would convert Paul's language into flimsy mirage or docetic
shadow.

The conflicting texts also play a key role in setting up the
paradoxical irony. By creating a textual tension in the description,
the conflicting texts promote the readers' suspicions of its literal
claim: how can Paul be both the paragon of weakness (4:9–13) and
the articulator of spirit and power (2:4); how can the Corinthians be
both not wise, powerful, nor eugenic (1:26) and yet prudent, strong,
and distinguished (4:10). Such tension functions creatively to
provoke the readers' involvement in the text and instigate efforts to
make sense of what, at first reading, can only be puzzling. The
tension challenges the reader beyond simple suspicion to consider
how Paul can be both powerful and powerless. If these texts raise the
readers' suspicions of the literal, they do so with the enticement to
seek out another universe of discourse—a second perspective—
within which they can receive the description meaningfully.

Iser's research helps us to understand the textual mechanism
which propels the reader from suspicion to an awareness of irony. In
his terminology, the conflicting texts create a "blank"—a break in
the connections which link the various textual segments—that the
readers must fill in their reading. Taking his cue from Virginia

Woolf's comment on Jane Austen—"She stimulates us to supply
what is not there"—Iser notes that through a text's blanks its reader

> is drawn into the events and made to supply what is meant
> from what is not said. What *is* said only appears to take on
> significance as a reference to what is not said; it is the
> implications and not the statements that give shape and
> weight to the meaning. But as the unsaid comes to life in
> the reader's imagination, so the said 'expands' to take on
> greater significance than might have been supposed.
> (1978:168)

In 1 Corinthians 1–4, the conflicting texts create a blank, forming a
gap in connection between the relative strength and weakness of
both Paul and the Corinthians. The text *says* that Paul displays
power, yet in affliction is powerless; that the Corinthians are prudent, strong, and distinguished, yet in their calling are not wise,
powerful or of status. The text does *not say*, but forces the reader to
supply, the connection between these features that allows him or
her to relate these features and transcend the confusion of their
literal conflict.

The presence of the blank incites the readers to seek a second
perspective in order to read 4:9–13 with meaningful connection to
the other textual segments.[18] However, the restoration of connectability, though crucial to the meaningful reading of Paul's text,
presents difficulty. As Iser suggests, the restoration depends upon
and coincides with the readers' "constitutive activity"—their capacity to interpret a text as a meaningful whole by imaginatively recon-
structing its patterns and relating its various segments—and for this
reason is indeterminate and far from inevitable (1978:180–231).

Readers might fail to restore 4:9–13 to its connectability with
the rest of Paul's discourse in at least two ways. First, they might
undercut the impetus for interpretation by simply ignoring the
blank and isolating 4:9–13 from the rest of the discourse. In abstraction from the challenge of the conflicting texts, 4:9–13 does not

---

[18] The break in consistency is not a mistake on the author's part, but an essential
literary mechanism by which the reader's bondage to familiar patterns of reading
and interpretation are broken. As Iser puts it, "such breaks act as hindrances to
comprehension and so force us to reject our habitual orientations as inadequate.
If one tries to ignore such breaks, or to condemn them as faults in accordance
with classical norms, one is in fact attempting to rob them of their function"
(1978: 18).

engage the readers' suspicion of the literal and, accordingly, invites a straightforward reading. Here the meaning of 4:9–13 would become clear, but also limited in scope, reduced to an item of information about Paul and the Corinthians. Without restored connectability 4:9–13 yet has meaning. But, in isolation from the rest of the discourse, that very clear meaning—Paul is weak and the Corinthians strong—does not approach the enlarged meaning stimulated in relation to the other segments and to "what is not said." Avoiding the blank produces a clear but meager meaning.

A second path to failure takes the blank with seriousness but never comes to terms with it. The limitations of the readers' "constitutive activity" or their unwillingness to release the text to the control of another perspective can frustrate restoration no less than can the abstraction of the text.[19] In this case, the reader surrenders the meaning of 4:9–13 to confusion. Again, the literal perspective dominates only, in this case, it achieves no clarity and causes the meaning of 4:9–13 to founder in contradiction with the conflicting texts. In either instance the failure to establish connectability impoverishes the reception of the text's full meaning: the first case results in a depletion of theme which arises from the tunnel-visioned concentration on the "theme of the moment" in isolation from other textual segments; the second case results in a diminution of the horizon of interpretation through myopic allegiance to the literal perspective.

The reader cannot fill the blank between 4:9–13 and the conflicting texts without broadening the horizon against which both can be reinterpreted. Where the text refuses to, the reader must supply the value of "strength" and "weakness" that enables them to be related in the description and in the conflicting texts. Here the text does not appear to tell its reader how to interpret its meaning, at least not directly. What is not given in theme, the reader must seek on the broader horizon.

The Quest for a Second Perspective: Seeking 'What is not There'

The readers' pursuit of 'what is not said' does not occur in a vacuum. At any particular point in the reading of a text, the earlier

---

[19] This failure, however, may also reflect a real inconnectability of the text. Frank Kermode's caution should be well taken: as modern readers we too quickly seek and impose a unity on texts whose genuinely fractured surface only mirrors the fortuities of life (64). Even here, though, the reader must construe some relationship among fractured pieces, if only to see that they are actually broken and thus grouped as those things which cannot be related.

stages of reading may influence the present activity. By the very sequencing of a text an author may predispose the readers "to supply what is not there" in a particular way. The author stimulates change in the readers' capacity to perceive and fill blanks as they move through the text. If the text has any power at all, the reader who begins its reading should differ from the one who finishes it. Accordingly, the author can prepare the way for the readers' restoration of the very connectability which the text fractures.

One way in which readers may fill a textual blank is by appropriating what an author has already provided in an earlier stage of the discourse. They may bridge the distance between any two segments by recollecting another perspective that remains accessible on the horizon. Thus, "what is not said"—the key to interpreting "strength" and "weakness"—readers may supply from "what already has been said" at an earlier point. The readers' task remains a creative act, only that creativity does not occur in a textual *tohu wabohu*. The accumulative reading of the text predisposes, but does not do away with, the readers' constitutive activity which may take the form of selecting from the various perspectives the one which illumines the particular blank.

Paul encourages the reader, when facing 4:9–13, to appropriate an already articulated perspective whose ironic features potentially enlarge the meaning of 4:9–13 and restore the text's connectability. In this way the text of 1 Corinthians 1–4 both manifests the puzzling creation of a blank and also suggests the way in which a reader might fill it. The discussion which follows details the perspective which Paul provides, showing how it is ironic, how Paul directs his readers to it, and how it enables the readers to confront the textual blank.

Paradoxical Irony: The Appropriation of 1:18–31

The perspective defined. Paul establishes the perspective of paradoxical irony in 1:18–31, a passage in which he articulates the implications of the cross-event. For Paul, God's scandalous activity in the cross founds a pervasive paradox that reverses not only the destiny of humankind, but transvalues the categories by which the reader understands that destiny. Paul's proclamation that the folly of the cross manifests God's power to save (1:18) refracts the definition of "folly" not to signify simply the absence of power, but to include within its bounds the presence of power. As a category, "folly" does not lose its moorings in the scandalous (1:23) nor sacrifice its equivalence to weakness and ignobility (1:26–28), but expresses precisely in its powerlessness, the value of power.

So too, Paul's proclamation fosters the perception of God's claim upon the foolish, weak, and insignificant features of life to empty the power of the wise, the strong, and the existent (1:27–28). In light of God's claim, "wisdom," "strength," and "existence" do not cease to be categories of power, but precisely the power which they signify expresses the value of powerlessness; "foolishness," "weakness," and "non-existence" retain their integrity as categories of powerlessness, but precisely in that powerlessness express the value of power. From this perspective the terms with which Paul describes himself and the Corinthians take on paradoxical meaning and become freighted with the understanding of God's activity in the cross.

The paradoxes of 1:18–31 manifest a complexity in their transvaluation of categories. Paul's "word of the cross," as 1:26–28 attests, moves in a double direction that expresses at once God's vindication of human powerlessness and humiliation of human power. Each of these movements, however, itself occurs paradoxically, giving to Paul's proclamation the features of a double paradox: God claims human "powerlessness" and shows it to be genuinely power; conversely, God opposes human "power" and shows it to be only powerlessness.[20]

The complexity becomes evident as the reader recognizes the quadratic dimensions of Paul's proclamation. Whereas the simple paradox requires the coexistence of two terms, Paul's proclamation expands to bring into play four terms. The reader of 1 Corinthians 1–4 cannot equate "power" and power or "powerlessness" and powerlessness for, in spite of their lexical kinship, their values differ dramatically. Nor can the reader reduce the complexity for Paul's perception of God's activity is thoroughly double-edged (even as it is paradoxical at each edge). God's call to salvation cannot empower the *klētoi* without also revealing their impotency. Such a complex word addresses the Corinthian predicament incisively, taking into account the need of the foolish, weak, and insignificant to be empowered, but also to be set free from the illusion of power which impoverishes them.

The perspective as ironic. Paul's articulation of the word of the cross introduces an ironic vantage point from which the terms of description in 4:9–13 lose their obvious value and self-evidence. The

---

[20] Here and following I use quotation marks to designate the reality that is paradoxically transformed; the absence of quotation marks signifies that which issues from the transformation.

text sharply contrasts the value that "strength" and "weakness" *appear* to have in the description and the value that they assume in the discourse. This contrast displays the characteristic features of paradoxical irony discussed earlier: the mechanism of paradox; the integrity of contrary terms; and their mutual qualification.

First, the mechanism of paradox pervades these verses. At the outset Paul identifies the word of the cross in terms of its coincident contraries: its articulation manifests both foolishness and the power of God (1:18). His initial formulation, however, tends to blur their paradoxical coincidence by designating a point of observation from which each contrary term is perceived: from the vantage point of the perishing, the word of the cross is seen as foolishness; from the vantage point of those being saved, divine power. Nevertheless, a genuine coincidence occurs. As understood in 1:21, God chooses precisely the foolishness of the kerygma to save the faithful. Their salvation does not occur apart from the foolishness of the kerygma and where that foolishness is proclaimed the faithful participate in salvation. Moreover, that salvation is concomitant with the recognition of the paradoxical character of the word. Paul does not envision the perishing and the saved to confront different realities such that the former face a powerless foolishness and the latter, an unfoolish power. Rather, Paul understands these groups to be separate only in that when confronting the same reality—the word of the cross—the perishing find *merely* foolishness, whereas those being saved perceive the paradox that this same foolishness is the power of God.

Virtually the same paradox recurs at 1:23–24, only in this case Paul has rendered "the word of the cross" as proclaiming a "crucified Messiah." Again, coincident contraries exist: to herald a crucified Messiah makes public a Christ who is both a stumbling block and foolishness as well as the power and wisdom of God. Here, also, Paul links particular features of the proclamation to distinct vantage points, but qualifies them in such a way as to rescue their coincidence. In 1:25, for instance, God's folly does not emerge from some Gentile angle of vision, such that only the uncalled *ethnoi* perceive it in the proclamation. That same folly surpasses human wisdom (1:25) and *is* God's own wisdom (1:21). Those who are called—both Jew and Greek[21]—do not circumvent the *skandalon* of proclaiming a crucified Christ, but instead perceive the paradox of doing so. In

---

[21] The replication of Jew and Greek on both sides of the paradox diminish the force of the point of observation as being a determinative matter.

heralding a crucified Messiah, the *klētoi* recognize the one who
became for them wisdom from God (1:30).

The discussion of the mechanism of paradox has already implied
the second feature of paradoxical irony, the integrity of terms. The
foolish, scandalous character of the word of the cross does not cloak
the power of God's activity only to fade away with the disclosure of
reality. Instead, it preserves the fabric of that reality and compels a
seriousness about it. Paul supplies a strong warrant for this being the
case by directing the Corinthians to their own calling (1:26), whose
powerless features, like those of the cross, God claims as the domain
of his activity. The Corinthians must give the scandalous features of
the cross their full due, for God has claimed none other than those
features as the contours of their call to salvation. For the Corinthians
(as Paul would want them to be), the scandal of the cross can be no
more a docetic dissimulation than can the call to salvation itself.

In paradoxical irony individual terms not only retain their integrity but mutually qualify each other, enlarging the meaning of any
given term. This third mark of paradoxical irony pervades 1:18–31,
but is especially evident at 1:27–28. These verses articulate the
implications of God's claim upon the world's regions of
powerlessness and bind together folly and wisdom, weakness and
strength, and the absence and presence of significance. Where this
is so, folly, for example, remains folly and signifies an absence of
wisdom, but never simply that. God's claim upon it enlarges its
meaning to include not only that which is less than the wisdom of
the world, but that which is greater. The interplay between expressed terms and the inclusion of their opposite values results in a
perpetual qualification that permits no term to mean simply itself.
The ironic vision of reality takes seriously the appearance of all
things, but remains suspicious of the apparent's capacity to define
the reality of any thing at all.

Recollecting the perspective. Ironic literature rarely gives so
explicitly the "second perspective" as does 1:18–31. Nevertheless,
even here, the reader confronts a certain subtlety. Paul sets his
articulation of the ironic perspective at some textual distance from
the description at 4:9–13. The detection of irony depends not on any
direct correlation of these texts by Paul, but on the reader's recollection of what Paul has already effected in the discourse. As Perelman
and Olbrechts-Tyteca have argued, the changes which a speaker or
writer effects on the audience at any given moment of the discourse
becomes part of the rhetorical situation for any subsequent stage of

the discourse (490–491). In this way 1:18–31 promotes a change in Paul's readers and becomes an important part of what they bring with them to the reading of 4:9–13. [22]

Admittedly, Paul does not instruct the readers to interpret 4:9–13 in terms of the word of the cross. He does, however, leave clues that he wants them to do so and predisposes them to undertake that task. One such clue is the vocabulary and conceptuality that Paul employs. An unmistakable parallelism exists between the antithetical terms of 4:10 and those of 1:27–28, involving either cognates or close synonyms. The earlier use of these terms conditions the readers' later reception of them and encourages their juxtaposition of these texts. Moreover, the common formal pattern— a sequence of three groups of contrasting terms—reenforces the parallelism and further incites the appropriation of 1:18–31 at the reading of 4:9–13.

Confronting the textual blank. While clear in certain of its parts, 1 Corinthians 1–4 as a whole has a "dark," enigmatic character which our textual blank exemplifies. [23] "What is said" in any one segment does not confuse until the shadow of another segment renders its meaning opaque. Then "what is not said" becomes paramount and compels the reader to enter the textual darkness of the blank in order to perceive the relationships which remain hidden in the brightness of the literal.

1 Corinthians 1–4 darkens at the point of the meaning of "weakness" and "strength." How are these terms to be understood such that their application to one and the same person or group does not cause the discourse to collapse in contradiction? A tacit Paul forces the readers to supply this understanding or appropriate it from another portion of the discourse. In doing so they meaningfully confront the textual blank.

The textual blank calls into question any one-dimensional interpretations of the world and the habit of constructing well-drawn boundaries to define and separate one item from another in that world. Such a style of envisioning reality expects clarity and consist-

[22] This does not mean that Paul's readers have been persuaded by him and adopted the reorientation that he calls for. It does mean, however, that their value-system has received a shock and that they cannot approach 4:9–13 with the same security that might otherwise have been possible. Whether convinced or not, the harsh echo of 1:18–31 still rings in their ears at the hearing of 4:9–13.
[23] See Kermode 23–49. Much of what Kermode says concerning the enigmatic character of narrative can also be seen in discursive texts that employ paradox.

ency. To perceive reality in this manner assumes that one thing is
one thing only and not another, that the various categories by which
persons, objects, and experiences are described have a basic univocity. A prominent instance of this way of perceiving the world is
reflected in the firm expectation that contrary categories, by definition, exclude each other. An item can be described by either one
category or its contrary, but not both at the same time. In this view,
the coexistence of contraries is a contradiction, a mistake.

Paul's discourse frustrates this style of perceiving reality by
forcing into the reader's attention the very thing which that orientation will not allow: the coexistence of contraries. Such an orientation
cannot allow, much less account for, the contrary description of Paul
and the Corinthians. Yet, precisely this contrary description Paul's
readers witness in the world of 1 Corinthians.

The perspective of paradoxical irony suggests another way of
perceiving reality that softens categorical boundaries instead of mor-
tifying them. When seen from this perspective, the meanings of
"strength" and "weakness" are transformed from mutual contradiction to a surprising point of identity: "strength" is weakness and
"weakness," strength. Here paradox challenges the readers' most
basic expectations not only of "strength" and "weakness" but of
reality itself and the ways it is to be perceived. The ironic perspective upends a familiar type of world-making, one that erects a world
with the rigid boundaries of univocity and frames all reality with the
constraints of consistency.

Paul's perspective allows readers to envision various segments of
the description not in terms of contradiction but as mutually-qualify-
ing aspects of a larger whole. Paradoxical irony integrates the
seemingly contradictory elements of description into a greater context of God's saving activity. Thus, in the case of Paul, the ironic
perspective does not allow the testimony of the conflicting texts to
disqualify his depiction in 4:9–13. Rather, the competing segments
work together to show that in the apostle's life, spirit and power
appear as they can only appear—through and as the fragile signs of
human weakness which God has claimed to nullify the force of
human strength, wisdom, and status (1:27–28). At the same time,
Paul's experience of weakness no longer expresses the unqualified
powerlessness of God's absence but signifies the power of God in the
midst of human powerlessness. The seemingly contradictory elements of description take on a new and reconciled meaning as the
terms of one paradox.

The case of the Corinthians is more complex. Through the tight parallelism between the terms of 4:10 and 1:26, Paul disposes the reader to subject his description of the Corinthians to the same paradoxical perspective that shaped his own portrayal. Yet here, to do so fails to unite the textual segments as obverse features of one paradox. The readers can unite the conflicting segments of Paul's self-description because they perceive the common value which "power" in 2:4 and his various weaknesses in 4:9–13 seem to share. Both express the "positive" value that reflects God's activity to bring life from human powerlessness. The context of 2:4 demonstrates that Paul's power is not the "power" which God overturns, "power" with a "negative" value, but the power that God brings forth from "weakness." Thus, Paul integrates the "power" of 2:4 into the same paradox that expresses the paradigmatic weakness to which God has called his apostle (4:9).

Paul, though, does not allow for the same integration of the Corinthian segments. Indeed, if he intends to reorient the Corinthians, he can scarcely afford to have his Corinthian readers harmonize the dissonance which prods that reorientation. Accordingly, the various segments of their description do not express a common value: as their close connection with the recital of God's saving activity (1:27–28) indicates, the various weaknesses of 1:26 have "positive" value; however, the Corinthian features of 4:10, given in antithesis to the "positive" value of the apostle's weakness express only a "negative" value. To be integrated into the one paradox the "power" of 4:10 would need to express the power which God sustains (as in 1:26) and not the "power" which God opposes and turns to weakness. Lacking the common value, Paul's paradoxical perspective does not unify the Corinthian description as much as polarize its segments.

The textual blank, when read against the foil of irony, manifests a certain asymmetry. In the case of Paul, the reader perceives that the apostle sees himself in one way, only a way whose paradoxical aspects must be described with a seeming duality. But in the case of the Corinthians, the reader sees that the apostle has portrayed them in two ways—the way of their calling (1:26) and the way of their self-perception (4:10)—each of which is subject to paradoxical reinterpretation.

If the paradoxical perspective vindicates the apostle by allowing the reader to see that weakness does not contradict the claim to power, it creates the opposite effect in the case of the Corinthians.

By polarizing the segments which describe the Corinthians Paul intends for his readers to see fully their contradiction and to be aware that the Corinthian calling and self-perception *cannot* be unified. Accordingly, Paul brings his Corinthian readers to a pressure point of question and not acquittal. As readers of Paul's text, the Corinthians must either deny the textual blank or accept its indictment. Paul has caught his readers in a dilemma: if they try to deny the blank they cease to be faithful readers of the letter; if they accept the text's judgment, however, they must repent their self-perception. The persisting blank here creates for the Corinthian readers the disorientation which initiates their reorientation.[24]

Before the enigma of the textual blank, the perspective of paradoxical irony offers to Paul's readers an enlargement of the meaning of "strength" and "weakness" that locates the descriptions of Paul and the Corinthians within the context of God's saving activity. Paradoxical interpretation, however, does not go so far as to make the blank to disappear. It does not make the inconsistent to be consistent, or that which is contrary to be any less so. Rather, it facilitates a reinterpretation of the categories such as "consistency" that, in turn, challenge a reader's expectations about the realities perceived through them. As such, paradoxical interpretation does not overcome the blank but, as with Kierkegaard's "nothingness," delicately plays with the presence of its emptiness and tames its capacity to terrify. In 1 Corinthians 1–4 the point is *not* that the terms "strength" and "weakness" cease to exist as contraries, but that they no longer threaten the reader with the absence of meaning or absurd contradiction: they no longer terrify. To assume the paradoxical perspective, on the one hand, is to confront the blank as the guardian of its emptiness and protector of its silence; but, on the other, it is to disover in "what is not said" not the absence of meaning, but its ironic presence.

THE PARADOXICAL SYSTEM OF VALUE

Systems of Value

No reader confronts a text innocently, but always understands it from some perspective which shapes and organizes the perception

---

[24] Note the similarity to the dynamic which Paul Ricoeur and others have identified in the parables of Jesus. See, e.g., Ricoeur, 1975.

of its meaning. The same holds true for the apprehension of reality or knowledge of a world. Neither "reality" nor "world" exists independently of the frames of reference which renders them perceptible and through which they assume particular contours. Nelson Goodman writes of this,

> If I ask about the world, you can offer to tell me how it is under one or more frames of reference; but if I insist that you tell me how it is apart from all frames, what can you say? We are confined to ways of describing whatever is described. Our universe, so to speak, consists of these ways rather than of a world or of worlds. (1978:2–3)

Taken in a broad sense, these frames of reference or "systems of value" provide a configuration of convictions which, according to Daniel Patte,

> imposes itself upon people and has the power of transforming unreality into reality for them. Presupposed by any cultural activity and by any discourse (profane as well as religious), these systems of convictions are the framework within which our discourses and our lives meaningfully unfold. They are, in Foucault's language, the conditions of the possibility of our discourses and lives. (1978:6)

The system of value reflects the fundamental framework through which one interprets reality. More particularly, the system of value structures the features of a world's reality in a given way, opposing and aligning what is greater and lesser, what is powerful and powerless, what is life-giving and death-dealing, what is real and illusory. Through its lens a world appears with a given contour. Not the namer of particular realities in that world, the system of value is the prior refraction of reality that brings the world into focus, ordering "the conditions of the possibility of our discourses and lives."

Every reader brings some system of value to the reading of a text. At the same time, however, every text brings into play its own system of value through which it communicates its vision of life. The text's system of value may or may not be congruent with that of its reader. To the extent that text and reader share a common system of value, the text will reenforce the convictions of the reader; to the extent that text and reader do *not* share such a system, the text will promote a change in the reader's convictions. The rhetorical context of 1 Corinthians 1–4 reflects this latter situation. Paul's discourse presupposes the construction of one system of value and the opposition to another which he has identified with the intended readers of the text. The system of value expressed through 1 Corinthians 1–4 is a thoroughly paradoxical one and reflects Paul's basic manner of apprehending the world over against the Corinthian rationality.

Paradox as System of Value

As a fundamental construal of reality, paradox markets no special definition of any particular item perceived within its scope. For instance, the paradoxical system of value creates no given definition of "strength" but takes whatever might be assumed of it and overturns those expectations, enlarging them to include the intimate presence of the contrary. As a construal of reality, the number of particular realities subject to its force is limitless, ranging from the most mundane of values to the most fundamental, life and death. Indeed, one cannot separate these, for the expression of any given paradox bears the freight of the entire paradoxical system of value.

The paradoxical system of value has an elusiveness which springs from the heart of its ongoing movement. Such a system can only be elusive for, by nature, paradoxes are "self-consuming," unable to stay at rest or halt the movement they begin.[25] One may affirm, for instance, the paradox that "weakness is strength" but cannot then reify it into the expectation that strength is guaranteed by its simple reversal. For if one defines "strength" as "weakness" then *that* expectation, albeit generated by a paradoxical reversal, is subject to another turn. A paradox can become a definition, a source of expectation, only at loss of its essential contrariety. In receiving reality as ordered by this paradoxical movement one still recognizes a structured world but, at the same time, takes heed of its provisional nature. In paraphrase of Peter Berger (69), the paradoxical world *does* have structure, only the constraints which give it shape are constructed of cardboard paper.

Ironic Convictions and Paradoxical Knowing

A system of value characteristically founds a way of perceiving the world and discerning reality, giving to its convictions an epistemological thrust. The paradoxical system of value expresses certain beliefs about the world that is to be known, but also indicates

---

[25] On self-consuming artifacts, see Fish, 1972.

how it is to be known. Five convictions which mark that way of knowing are as follows:

1. *The paradoxical system of value presupposes and creates a sense of open-ended reality.* The reality of the paradoxical world does not exist as a continuous whole; its topography, uneven and fragmented, cannot be traversed through any direct, unbroken route or charted with clear boundaries. In its open-endedness the paradoxical world displays an enigmatic darkness that inspires the curious to penetrate its shadows—to know what has not been disclosed—but fates that attempt to be a provisional and partial apprehension. Paradoxical knowing aims not at the dis-*closure* of the world as a continuous whole, but seeks a pervasive openness to the world in its fullest, and thus, partially undisclosed, reality.

2. *The reality which one perceives within the paradoxical system of value has a relational and systemic character.* Paradoxical knowing seeks the relation between particular realities and the way they function together in a common world. Because the features of the paradoxical world have no independence from one another, the attempt to know that world atomistically is doomed to fail. Paradoxical knowing can only be an apprehension of a relationship.

3. *The paradoxical system of value obligates its knower to preserve the multi-dimensionality of reality.* The paradoxical world is both what it appears to be and yet is always other than it appears to be. Accordingly, the attempt to know it must transcend the blinders of one-dimensionality, be those in the form of a literal, exclusive focus on the apparent or the dissimulative, strict focus on the non-apparent. Paradoxical knowing aims to see the world in the complexity of its plural dimensions.

4. *Paradoxical knowing has an interrogative character.* The paradoxical world presents itself as a question. Like a riddle, the "blanks" of the paradoxical world require one to grasp reality through an on-going process of reinterpretation. The paradoxical world lacks self-evidence and remains critical of the idolatry of definition. No answer to an already formulated puzzle of reality, paradox reformulates the puzzle, challenging the knowers' assumptions about reality including the questions that can be asked of it.

5. *Paradoxical knowing spawns an epistemology of surprise.* One can perceive the paradoxical world only with a radical openness to the unexpected. That which distorts the perception of reality, leading knowers to confuse the unreal for the real, is primarily fixed expectations about what real-

ity must consist of and what forms it must take. Paradoxical
knowing subverts expectations so that the knower, caught in
surprise, is brought to a point of openness in an enlarged
world.

These five convictions promote an ironic contrast between what
knowing would appear to involve and what it actually entails in the
paradoxical world. Paradoxical knowing brings into question the
familiar project of knowledge for it yields not positive knowledge
about anything, only an awareness of not-knowing. Neither the
conditions for knowledge nor its results resemble what one would
expect of knowing: that is, paradoxical knowledge does not lead to
any security of what is known, but to an openness to what is not
known; does not yield the clarity of definition, but the tangled
dialectic of relation; does not allow for the banishment of confusion,
but values its appreciation of the complexity of reality; does not
furnish an answer to anything, but only a question to all things; and
does not give birth to any predictability about the world, only a
pervasive sense of awaiting its surprise.

Although the implications of these convictions go well beyond
the issue of 1 Corinthians, we should take note here of what is at
stake for our understanding of the Corinthian controversy. At its
most basic dimensions the controversy reflects the different ways
which Paul and the Corinthians apprehend reality: their conflict is
fundamentally epistemological.

The paradoxical character of Paul's gospel expresses the convictions detailed above and, when expressed within the Corinthian
controversy, serves Paul's apologetic and homiletic goals. To defend
himself against perceived criticism of his authority Paul must relo-
cate its issue away from any closed, one-dimensional constraints that
would undermine it at the outset. He must break the hold of the
Corinthian system of value and its one-dimensional assumption that
"weakness is (only) weakness" if he is to reopen the issue of authority. By placing his weakness within an open-ended system Paul
calls into question any predetermination of its implications, especially the anticipated Corinthian judgment that his plight sig-
nified a lack of power and authority. By closely tying his weakness to
a paradoxical strength, Paul makes it impossible for his readers to
assimilate his discourse to any preconceived world of one-dimension
and suggests the inadequacy of such a perspective to discern the
contours of God's calling. Moreover, the force of such frustration,
while taking away the Corinthian expectation of the world, leaves

them all the more vulnerable to the surprising manifestations of God's power. Paul can neither defend himself nor reorient the Corinthians within the constraints of a one-dimensional way of knowing; only the way of paradox will suffice.

Paradoxical Hermeneutics: " 'There are Elephants All The Way Down' "

The convictions of the paradoxical system of value point to an instability in the ironic universe, an instability which may be that world's most prominent feature. With Wayne Booth,

> At last we cross that formidable chasm . . .—the fundamental distinction between stable ironies and ironies in which the truth asserted or implied is that no stable reconstruction can be made out of the ruins revealed through the irony. The author . . . refuses to declare himself, however subtly, *for* any stable proposition, even the opposite of whatever proposition his irony vigorously denies. The only sure affirmation is that negation that begins all ironic play: "this affirmation must be rejected." (1974:240)

The resulting situation Booth likens to the proverbial teaching of the Eastern sage

> who taught that the world rests on the back of an elephant, which in turn stands on the back of another elephant. When one of his disciples finally took courage and asked him what *that* elephant stands on, he confided, "There are elephants *all the way down*." (1974:243)

The instability of the paradoxical world is that one irony stands on another such that 'there are ironies all the way down.'[26]

One cannot easily deny the instability of paradoxical irony. We should not, however, conclude from this instability that irony permits no world of meaning. The self-consuming character of the paradoxical world differs from the nihilistic and absurd chaos in

---

[26] Kierkegaard's discussion of irony as "infinite absolute negativity" gives a version of the same phenomenon (see, e.g., 276). His portrayal of Socrates' ironic behavior describes the effect of this instability: "This tactic (the use of irony) he maintained to the last, a fact which was especially apparent when he stood accused. But his zeal in its service consumed him, and at last he, too, was seized with irony: everything spins round him, he becomes giddy, and all things lose their reality" (281).

which neither meaning nor concern have any place. One can push paradox beyond its own limits and into absurdity but, at the same time, paradox *does* have a limit beyond which it cannot go without sacrificing its identity as paradox. The instability of the paradoxical world expresses unceasing movement, but never without a certain control. Like a delicately improvised dance, paradox pursues its own unexpected steps and surprising turns, but never without rhythm.

The unceasing movement of paradox steadily guards the domain of the unexpected from those who would arrest its pendular reversals. Where the open-endedness of paradox insures the freedom of ongoing reversal—the possibility of the unexpected—the rhythm of paradox asserts itself as a reliable structure or limit: the reversal *must* occur. No item can escape the constraining intimacy of its contrary. Like the prophet who destroys the people's idols before a God who is "other", paradox shatters the hold of conventional expectation and points to a single deity, the truth of the unexpected. No simple chaos holds sway in the paradoxical world, for in its sphere one can count on the intrusion of surprise. This is the rhythm that controls the dance of paradox, even as it is the undying pulse whose beat lets no foot be still.

As its legacy paradox bequeaths a hermeneutic of life, a projection of a world whose elusive gift of reality is always and only a way of knowing reality.[27] Kierkegaard, keenly aware of the instability of paradoxical irony, can yet speak of it as a *way* and does so instructively:

> Irony is like the negative way, not the truth but the way.
> Everyone who has a result merely as such does not possess
> it, for he has not the way. When irony appears on the scene
> it brings the way, though not the way whereby one who
> imagines himself to have a result comes to possess it, but
> the way whereby the result forsakes him. (340)

So, too, Wayne Booth, in wrestling with the ironic instability of Plato and Socrates, cannot interpret them to be either without knowledge or in firm possession of it, but speaks of their knowledge of a *method:*

> No one can read many Platonic dialogues without becoming
> convinced of Plato's conviction that he and Socrates both

[27] Here consider the insight of John Barth's provocative aphorism: "the key to the treasure is the treasure." (64)

know a good deal. For one thing . . . *they know a method.*
They know that every statement of truth can be questioned
from *some* point of view. (1974: 274)

If by nothing else, the way and method of irony—that there is a
way and method, no matter how undisclosed—distinguish it from
the chaotic nihilism that proclaims the collapse of meaning and
conviction. The world which Paul projects is not a valueless world in
which "strength" and "wisdom" have lost all meaning, but a world in
which that meaning must be discovered in a particular way—the
way of paradox that demands openness and risks the surprise of
reversal.

Paul's paradoxical irony resembles what Booth has found amid
the instability of Peter Weiss' *Marat/Sade:*

> when Weiss' troupe of madmen come marching toward the
> spectators at the end of *Marat/Sade*, they are disconcerted
> not with a sense that nothing matters to Weiss, but that he is
> asking them to care for a great deal without offering the
> usual helps. (1974:250)

Paul's irony strives to provoke the reader's attention to the realities
manifest in the paradoxical world of God's calling, a world that
matters. As a way of knowing, paradox is always "without the usual
helps" for the ironist believes that those "usual helps" obscure the
reality of that which matters decisively. Vision, the capacity to see
reality, is not destroyed by paradox but restored and enlarged. To
see only that "there are elephants all the way down" is yet to see and
moreover to discover the lens through which the surprising world of
God's calling comes unexpectedly into focus.

Chapter IV

THE LANGUAGE OF AFFLICTION: FORCEFUL AND IMAGINATIVE STYLE

> In all eternity it is impossible for me to compel a person
> to accept an opinion, a conviction, a belief. But one thing
> I can do: I can compel him to take notice.
>
> SØREN KIERKEGAARD
> *The Point of View for My Work
> as an Author*

PLAIN SPEECH AND FORCEFUL AND IMAGINATIVE LANGUAGE

We cannot understand the rhetorical effect of Paul's irony apart from considering the language which implements it. In order to do so we will take note of the contrast between two dimensions of language that a text may express and emphasize. Following Robert Tannehill, we will refer to these dimensions as those of "plain speech" and "forceful and imaginative language" (see 11–37).[1]

Plain speech accents the denotative, informational dimension of a text. Marked by its straightforward character, plain speech enables a text to communicate certain data with clarity and precision. By contrast, forceful and imaginative language emphasizes the connotative, symbolic dimension of a text.[2] Shaped by the constraints of

---

[1] The distinction does not originate with Tannehill who himself expresses indebtedness to Philip Wheelwright's reflections on "steno-" and "tensive" language. Also note that the distinction is common in the rhetorical and stylistic handbooks of antiquity, e.g., Demetrius, *De Elocutione* 36. Tannehill's exposition, however, remains significant in its emphasis of the respective functions (the reader-effects) of these dimensions of language and in its consideration of the role of imagination vis-a-vis these dimensions.

[2] Thus Patte and Patte: 3. Although the Pattes here follow Tannehill's basic distinction, they modify it noting that the distinction is a relative one in any given text. The denotative and connotative dimensions which plain speech and symbolic speech respectively communicate both exist in any one text, but each

formal pattern and tension and distinguished by the soft focus of its
metaphoric diction, such language can only obscure the informational dimension of the text. Yet it effectively engages the readers so
that they perceive more fully the symbolic value of the text, its
vision of life. Of forceful and imaginative language, Patte writes:

> Its function is not the communication of data but the com-
> munication of visions of life and the world. It opens a
> window upon the realm of feelings (which manifest the
> values that we spontaneously attach to the interrelationship
> of the innumerable facets of human experience) and upon
> the realm of the imagination (through which we perceive
> the fundamental purposefulness and meaningfulness of life).
> The main function of symbolic speech is the awakening of
> the imagination by challenging (or eventually reinforcing)
> the vision of life and of the world that we hold . . . This
> imaginative language is also qualified by Tannehill as being
> "forceful"; it has the *power* to awaken the imagination, the
> power to "touch the depths from which our personal visions
> of life arise". (1978:3)

While every text has both an informational and a symbolic
dimension, the contrast between the modes of language which
illumines these dimensions is sharp. Because it intends to communicate information with precision, plain speech retains a one-dimensionality, a flat character designed to build no obstructions to the
reader's reception of the text. Accordingly, plain speech exercises a
neutral impersonality that allows readers to receive it passively
while remaining secure in their personal orientations of self and
world. The narcotic blandness of plain speech does not penetrate the
reader's sense of self and has no intention of doing so. To disturb that
sense of self can only obstruct the smooth flow of information, for
while the informational dimension of a text cannot engage the
reader's orientation, it yet depends upon some such system of value
out of which its data can be assessed. Plain speech lulls its readers.
Where deliberately exercised, its advocate knows that readers cannot focus on information while feeling the symbolic ground beneath
their feet start to shake.

---

style emphasizes one dimension while suppressing the other. In principle one
can construe Shakespeare as "information" or a phone book as poetry, but to do
so is to read against the intentionality of the language. For further discussion of
this distinction with regard to biblical language see Heschel, 178–80.

Forceful and imaginative language (or, symbolic speech), however, engages its readers profoundly in their personal orientation. To block the path of any impersonal reading, symbolic speech exercises language "with the volume turned way up" (Tannehill 63). Its increased intensity and immediacy heighten the readers' affectivity such that the reading becomes unavoidably personal.[3] Where plain speech is flat, symbolic speech shows multi-dimensionality, creating ambiguity and tension; where plain speech seeks clarity, symbolic speech sets in action images whose soft focus and connotative thrust arrest its reader; where plain speech narcotizes the reader's personal orientation, leaving it intact as firm ground on which to receive information, symbolic speech shakes that ground by stimulating the imagination from which other such orientations emerge. Forceful and imaginative language appropriates the reader's experience of the text for its own purposes. Through the awakening of the imagination, symbolic speech makes of its readers forces which resist the reading of the text as information. Said more positively, symbolic speech enables a text to generate the readers' creation of new visions of life and promotes a transformation of deep convictions.

THE SELF-DESCRIPTION OF AFFLICTION AS SYMBOLIC SPEECH

At no time in the discourse does Paul employ the language of affliction simply to communicate the datum that he is weak. In the first place, he has no need to do so. His perception of the climate of criticism presupposes that the Corinthians already have this infor-

---

[3] The affective nature of symbolic speech forces the reader to "feel" something in the reading of the text. What is experienced in that reading becomes an event in the existence of the reader and holds the capacity to transform the reader's previously held understanding of existence. In this way the world of a text intersects the world of the reader. H. Richard Niebuhr, reflecting on the way in which an event becomes revelatory, argues similarly (1974). For Niebuhr, an event is revelatory (i.e., has power) only when it is remembered as an event not in impersonal time (external history), but in "our history" (internal history). The "plain speech" rendering of external history and the symbolic evocation of internal history point to a difference not in the event itself—any event, like any text has both denotative and connotative dimensions—but in its narration, the style which keeps it distant as an event in impersonal time, or brings it near as an event to be experienced as "our history." Note especially Niebuhr's contrast between the Gettysburg Address (symbolic speech) and the account of the Declaration of Independence in the *Cambridge Modern History* (plain speech) (1974:44–45).

mation. Secondly, the underlying ironic perspective of the discourse allows innocence to none of Paul's statements concerning weakness. The apostle's most unpretentious diction yet lacks anything resembling straightforwardness.

The symbolic character of Paul's language of affliction intensifies in his description of apostolic life at 4:9–13. Paul's readers receive no new information at this point for the description echoes what Paul has already said about himself: the apostle is weak, powerless, subject to affliction. Instead, Paul's language takes a forceful turn that goes beyond the earlier concessions of weakness. No longer does his reference to weakness resemble simple acknowledgement of its existence, as is the case with the relatively unassuming language of 2:3. Now Paul concedes his weakness with increased volume:

> For I think God has put us apostles on display as the lowest of all people, like those who are condemned to death, because we have become a spectacle to the world, to angels, and human beings. We are fools for the sake of Christ, but you are sensible in Christ; we are weak, but you are strong; you are held in esteem, but we have no honor. Up to the present moment we hunger and thirst and lack clothing and are beaten and wander about and labor, working with our own hands. When abused, we bless; when persecuted, we accept; when slandered, we relent. We have become the world's scum, the refuse of all things until now. (4:9–13)

The proliferation of literary devices in these verses marks this text as an instance of forceful and imaginative language. As Paul gives pattern to his description through antithetical parallelism and chiasm and creates nuance with repetition, hyperbole, and imagery, he stresses the connotations of weakness. If Paul ever was concerned to report the fact of his weakness he has here abandoned such an attempt and has set out to use the language of affliction to assault the Corinthian sensibility. Not merely instrumental, the language of affliction continues to express Paul's own convictions about God's activity in the world. But conviction addresses conviction and thereby challenges those systems of value which stand over against its own. In conflict Paul's rhetoric becomes a potent weapon to break down the readers' defenses, leaving their visions of life unguarded and vulnerable to change.

The power of Paul's discourse grows primarily from its ironic system of value. However, in 4:9–13 Paul creates a forceful text from more than irony alone. He has at his disposal a full arsenal of literary devices through which he augments his irony and implements its elements with a fuller engagement of the reader. Paul's style helps to make his fundamental irony effective and forceful.

The Rhetorical Demand for Symbolic Speech

Interpreters of Paul's letters have commonly noted the occasional character of these texts, recognizing the influence of particular contexts on the meaning of each letter. From this recognition one moves easily and appropriately to the corollary that Paul does not intend to craft canonical documents but to offer a "word on target" in a given time and place. While these observations seem beyond dispute, some caution is yet warranted in discerning their implication for the understanding of Paul's language.

No one can accuse Paul of writing clearly. Read in light of the expectations of plain speech—that he intends to communicate information—Paul's letters are obscure and difficult. To echo Wayne Booth, Paul's reader justly raises the question, "Why don't you say what you mean?" (1978:1–13). Is it because Paul writes poorly, lacking the skill to communicate clearly the information he would give to his communities?[4] Is it because he writes with "teary eyes" (2 Cor. 2:4) or like a madman (2 Cor. 11:21), letting his personal involvement hinder his capacity to write with control? Or does the confusion in his language derive from a situational pressure whose urgency compels him to write with less caution and reserve than he might have under other conditions?

With some truth one may answer "yes" to each of these questions, but such answers fail to explain why Paul does not say simply what he means. Each of these responses would assume that Paul intends to communicate plainly but is prevented from doing so by the limitations of his ability or of the situation. Another view, which

---

[4] Cf. Deissmann's observation that the letters of Paul lack rhetorical, artistic features; that is, that Paul's writings are genuinely letters and not epistles (1911:290–302 and 1957:12). Deissmann would suggest that Paul's letters belong in the category of "plain speech." The question would remain, however, as to whether they provide a good use of that style. Note also recent studies examining the question of Paul's education, particularly whether or not he is rhetorically trained; see Malherbe 34–35 and 45; and Judge 1960–61:4–15 and 125–37; 1972:19–36.

we will support for our text, is that the situation *does* shape Paul's language but *not* by hampering his ability to write clearly. The rhetorical situation does not prevent Paul from communicating clearly; *it prevents him from wanting to*.

The rhetorical situation of 1 Corinthians 1–4 demands Paul's use of symbolic speech. To vindicate his authority Paul must coincidentally change the Corinthian system of value. Accordingly, to provide more data about his claims to authority or his weakness, no matter how clearly presented, would inevitably miss the mark. The rhetoric of plain speech could only be ineffective for the Corinthians would interpret its information in terms of their own problematic orientation. In its "plainness" and clarity such rhetoric lacks the power to challenge a system of value. Of this Tannehill writes:

> Plain speech is good for communication within established interpretations of the world but it bypasses the imagination and so has little power to change these fundamental interpretations . . . The communication of plain speech will be accepted as an "idea" and placed in the pigeonhole where it will least disturb our basic vision of self and world. Or it will be accepted as a rule of behavior without affecting the basic orientation of the self. This will happen if the discourse permits it, for our basic visions show that they are basic by secretly determining our evaluation of everything else. Plain speech does permit this and so permits acceptance on the intellectual level, without any corresponding change in the self, or acceptance as a rule of behavior, without any change in the self's goals. Both are ways in which we protect ourselves against the threat of change. (27)

The rhetorical situation requires that Paul do whatever possible to prevent the Corinthians from receiving his language as an idea to be "pigeonholed" within their customary system of value. He must avoid the rhetoric of plain speech because, in its clarity, it would emphasize the denotation of the discourse and frame Paul's weakness as another item of information to be processed in the usual way. At best, this would misread the problem: Paul and the Corinthians agree on the denotation, that he is weak, but fundamentally disagree on its connotation. More likely, any emphasis on Paul's weakness as such, without any accompanying change in conviction, would only aggravate his rejection. If Paul were simply to say what he means he would let go unchecked, if not give tacit approval to, the Corinthian system of value. He would permit the roots of the problem to deepen and grow sturdy.

If the rhetorical situation discourages the use of plain speech, it encourages that of symbolic speech. Through the use of symbolic speech a writer taps the potential of language to estrange ordinary images and notions from their expected contexts, thereby jolting readers out of familiar continuities. Arrested by the novelty of symbolic speech, its readers are diverted from their well-defended patterns of thinking and may find that their perception of new insight now blocks any retreat into the familiar system of value. For Paul to meet his rhetorical goals he must depend on such a use of language to shock his readers out of their habitual orientation and render them vulnerable to his irony.

Symbolic speech promotes the readers' involvement in the text. The shock value of symbolic speech does not originate with the readers' detached reflection, but from the more immediate engagement of their sensibility and affections. Symbolic speech *does* something to the readers and forces them to respond not with calculation but with immediacy. Like a sudden blow to the stomach or the unexpected echo of a once-treasured song, effective symbolic speech catches its readers off-guard. It causes its readers to respond in spite of what they think or before they can withdraw into more considered reflection about what they have read. Symbolic speech is experienced before interpreted. As Paul deploys this language he builds from the readers' experience of the text a roadblock to their rationality and the interpretation that issues from it. If only for the moment, the expression of such language initiates Paul's vindication and the Corinthian reorientation.

The Rhetorical Function of Paul's Literary Devices

Through patterns and images a text discloses an intention to emphasize connotation and takes on a forceful character. Paul's self-description of apostolic life exemplifies this in its use of antithesis, repetition, and imagery. These devices engage Paul's readers in their personal orientation and thus play a vital role in his rhetorical strategy.

Antithesis
Through antithesis an author expresses a contrast in meaning and gives it emphasis with a parallel in the grammatical structure itself. Paul uses this patterned contrast when he writes, "We are fools for the sake of Christ, but you are sensible in Christ; we are

weak, but you are strong; you are held in esteem, but we have no honor" (4:10).[5] This chain of antitheses has several effects upon Paul's readers as they confront his self-description.

First, because of its "attentional novelty," the antithetical form emphasizes and makes memorable Paul's concern about his weakness and the Corinthian strength.[6] The antithetical form draws the readers' attention by displaying a pattern that stands out from the ordinary flow of speech or from the pattern of the preceding text. Through the novelty of its pattern, Paul's antithetical statements are brought into the foreground of the readers' scope. Both by structuring his concern into some pattern and by utilizing the capacity of that particular pattern to stand out from its textual background, Paul has taken steps to insure that his reader will notice and remember his comments on weakness and strength.

Second, the antithetical form brings into play the capacity of the elements so patterned to become mutually interpretive. Following Brandt, antithesis does more than simply accent the elements in its pattern; it contributes to their definition. He writes, "When I say not this, but that, I am not merely emphasizing a difference, I am setting up a class within which a distinction is being made, and hence I am significantly contributing to the concept by the alternatives I reject" (161). Thus, apostolic weakness is *not* Corinthian strength; Corinthian honor is *not* apostolic dishonor. Paul fashions the portraits of apostolic life and of the Corinthian sensibility in part through the clustered associations of parallel terms (e.g., "foolishness," "weakness," "dishonor"); however, he also creates these portraits by opposing terms which allows the reader to envision what something is in relief to what it is not.

Where drawn sharply, the mutually interpretive relation can take the form of mutual exclusion. To interpret Paul's weakness antithetically is to exclude from its domain the antithetical comple-

---

[5] Noting this and numerous other instances of patterned contrast, Weiss (1897:13–19 and 1970:411–15) and Bultmann (79–80) pointed to antithesis as a prominent feature of Pauline rhetoric. More recently Schneider has studied the various Pauline antitheses with an eye to their formal classification. These studies focus primarily on the historical background and form of Paul's antitheses, but do not comment upon their rhetorical function.

[6] R. Carpenter, in discussing the "attentional novelty" of antithesis, writes: "Human beings characteristically develop expectations about what would be customary and familiar in a given situation; and when a stimulus is discrepant with those expectations, it is novel and tends to be noticed and remembered until successive or prolonged appearances decrease its saliency" (428–29).

ment, Corinthian strength. The form forces the readers to make a choice as to which side of the antithesis they will affirm and insists that in doing so they give up the complement. By his antithetical pairings Paul prevents the reader from coincidentally affirming both the call to apostolic existence and the Corinthian sensibility.

Because of its capacity for mutual exclusion, the antithetical form adapts well to situations of controversy. Its literary structure may mirror an already existing conflict or, in its demand for the readers' decision, may precipitate controversy. A new orientation cannot emerge without calling into question the prevailing orientation. Accordingly, if the antithesis promises something new, it yet demands the giving up of something familiar and thus incites controversy. Tannehill writes, "In antithesis the prevailing perspective is allowed expression so that it can be challenged, and the new perspective appears over against it. Thus the hearer is prevented from subsuming the new perspective under the old. It is this clash of perspectives that is revelatory" (1975:54). Paul's antitheses work to convince his readers that what he says about apostolic life cannot be subsumed under the Corinthian sensibility. In form they call for the readers' decision.

In addition to its roles of emphasis and definition, the antithetical form displays a third function: the creation of a certain expectation in the readers that encourages their assent to the antithesis. Where expressed as a series, antitheses generate a predictability that disposes the reader to complete the sequence at the mention of the first element of the pair. Once the readers discern a pattern they read with expectation of the pattern's fulfillment. Thus, when Paul initiates the pattern, "we are fools. . . , but you are sensible. . . ," he leads the reader to expect that he will follow "we are weak" with "you are strong." This expectation persuades. Given the basic symmetry of antithetical structure, the reader not only expects the completion of the pattern, but desires it, at least at the formal level, and assents to the rhythm of the form. Formal assent places the readers in tandem with the author, even where, on other grounds, they might wish only to disagree. Moreover, formal assent encourages acceptance of the material associated with it. As Kenneth Burke has noted,

> Once you grasp the trend of the form, it invites participation
> regardless of subject matter. Formally you will find yourself
> swinging along with the succession of antitheses, even

though you may not agree with the proposition that is being presented in this form. Or it may even be an opponent's proposition which you resent—yet for the duration of the statement itself you might "help him out" to the extent of yielding to the formal development, surrendering to the symmetry as such. Of course, the more violent your original resistance to the proposition, the weaker will be your degree of "surrender" by "collaborating" with the form. But in cases where a decision is still to be reached, a yielding to the form prepares for assent to the matter identified with it. Thus, you are drawn to the form, not in your capacity as a partisan, but because of some "universal" appeal in it. And this attitude of assent may then be transferred to the matter which happens to be associated with the form. (Cited by Carpenter 434–35)

Following this perspective, Paul can be seen to promote his readers' acceptance of the incommensurability between the Corinthian orientation and his own. By drawing them into an antithetical pattern whose structured rhythm inclines their "willing completion" of the sequence, he encourages their collaboration in his own convictions. In light of the close connection between Paul's depiction of apostolic life (4:10) and his earlier casting of the Corinthian calling (1:26), the antitheses of 4:10 seduce the Corinthian readers to affirm the distance between their self-perception and the portrayed reality of their calling.

The effects of antithesis show the signs of forceful and imaginative discourse. Because of its patterned structure an antithetical text denies the readers' detachment and entices their involvement in the reading process. Should the readers withdraw to digest the text's denotation, the persistent "tapping of the feet" at the text's pulse gives the lie to their attempt to do so. Accented and prominent in the textual foreground, the readers cannot ignore the passage; highly memorable in structure, they cannot easily forget it; engaging in its pattern, they cannot read it without also giving assent to its completion. In short, Paul has caused his readers' experience of the text to stand in the way of construing it as an item of information to be processed (and thus dismissed) through the constraints of their given rationality.

Repetition
Repetition has the potential either to heighten the forcefulness of a text or to diminish whatever power it may otherwise have

expressed. On the one hand, when carried to great length and expressed without variety, repetition can become monotonous and dull the sensitivity of the reader. Such an effect, typical of long lists, emphasizes the denotation of its elements by reducing them to a common item in a series. On the other hand, when combined with sensitivity to patterned contrast and imaginative diction, repetition can allow a text to become more engaging and to increase its affectivity. As used, for instance, in poetic texts, repetition emphasizes repeated elements and utilizes the reader's sense of expectation in creating its meaning. Emphasis and expectation point the readers to the text's connotations, signalling to them that the text intends to do more than communicate information about its items.

A writer can achieve effective repetition in various ways. Most obviously, he or she can simply repeat given words or phrases, creating a sense of verbal repetition. Such repetition might be immediate, directly following the utterance to be repeated, or might occur at some interval. A striking example of both can be seen in the second of Denise Levertov's "Three Meditations":

> Who was it yelled, cracking
> the glass of delight?
> Who sent the child
> sobbing to bed, and woke it
> later to comfort it?
> I, I, I, I,
> I multitude, I tyrant,
> I angel, I you, you
> world . . .

Here the poet's verbal repetition of the interrogative "who" and its pronominal answer, "I," creates a powerful exchange that does not allow the reader's attention to stray from the poem's indictment and assault on the self of the "I".

Not all repetition, however, repeats words and phrases. An author can create repetition by establishing a recurring syntactical or formal pattern. For instance, Matthew's version of the "Lord's Prayer" initiates a repetitive pattern by beginning its first three petitions with third-person singular imperatives:

> *hagiasthēto to onoma sou*
> *eltheto hē basileia sou*
> *genēthēto to thelēma sou* (6:9–10)

The similar endings of both the verbs and nouns, the persistent position and symmetry of the subjects, the recurrence of the second-person, singular pronoun at the conclusion of each petition, combine to create a forceful sense of repetition that is primarily syntactical, yet reenforced by the repetition of sound, rhythm, and word. Paul uses repetition extensively in 4:9–13, yet his particular use of it varies from verse to verse. In the self-description the patterns of repetition fall into three distinct sections: the antitheses contrasting apostles and Corinthians (4:10); the polysyndetic series of apostolic hardships (4:11–12a); and the chain of apostolic responses to conditions imposed upon them (4:12b–13).

We have already discussed at some length the antitheses of 4:10 and here need only add that Paul perpetuates the antithetical pattern through the repetition of contrasting pairs. What enables the reader to perceive a pattern is the recurrence of its form, in our text the three-fold repetition of the contrasting pairs. The verbal markers of that pattern—Paul's repetition in each instance of contrasting personal pronouns—facilitate the readers' discernment of the pattern and act to punctuate its rhythm.[7]

Through the six-fold repetition of the conjunction "*kai*," Paul forges the chain of hardships which marks the second section of repetition:

> *kai peinōmen kai dipsōmen kai gymniteuomen kai kolaphizometha kai astatoumen kai kopiōmen.* (4:11–12a)

Verbally, Paul repeats the conjunction "*kai*" before citing each hardship, a repetition that punctuates and sets off each element in the series, yet links them together as elements in a common sequence. At the same time, the verbal repetition reflects a recurring polysyndetic syntax that expresses a pattern of alternating conjunctions and first-person, plural verbs. This syntactical pattern gives to the text a

---

[7] The verbal markers *(hēmeis/humeis)* also point to Paul's alteration of the pattern in the third instance. Whereas in the first two pairs Paul moves from first person to second person, in the third he reverses the order. In one sense the demands of transition motivate the reversal: the reader progresses more smoothly to the first-person sequence of apostolic hardships if the previous sequence has cadenced in the first-person. In another sense, though, the variance is needed to guard against the potential of the pattern to lull the reader into inattentiveness. The alteration has "attentional novelty," issuing in a chiasm which itself creates a pattern of alternate stress.

sense of phonic repetition; insofar as five of the six verbs share a common ending, the reader *hears* the repetition and feels the force of its rhythm. The polysyndetic repetition shapes the readers' apprehension of Paul's weakness. By scattering the expression of his weakness through the series of afflictions, Paul forces the readers to linger on the experience and contemplate it in concrete form. Where the readers might wish to place weakness at a distance, Paul brings it near by tying it to diverse, but particular hardships. Instead of confronting an abstract weakness, the readers face the apostle's hunger and thirst. Where they might hope to hurry past the problematic area of the apostle's affliction, Paul slows down the progress of their thought. The controversial weakness does not vanish from the readers' horizon as soon as it has been expressed. On the contrary, it surfaces repeatedly.

In addition, the polysyndetic repetition creates an impression of extensiveness that implies to the reader that Paul's weakness embraces a wide breadth of human affliction. Paul's list of hardships does not exhaust the catalog of apostolic miseries yet, through repetition, it implies more than it specifically names. The repetition creates in the reader the expectation that the series could continue if Paul chose to prolong the matter. As specific cases in point, the named hardships do not encompass the whole of Paul's weakness, but are only its symptoms.

Following the series of hardships, Paul gives a series of apostolic responses in the face of adverse conditions:

> *loidoroumenoi eulogoumen,*
> *diōkomenoi anechometha,*
> *dysphēmoumenoi parakaloumen* (4:12b–13)

This third section of repetition displays both syntactical and phonic repetition. Syntactically, Paul creates a recurring pattern of contrasting pairs, each pair constituted by an adverbial, passive participle (the adverse condition) and a first-person plural, indicative verb (the apostolic response). The phonic repetition that occurs through the common word-endings (*-menoi* and *-oumen*) and accented vowel-sounds (*o* and *ou*) reenforces the syntactical pattern. The effect of this pattern continues the force of Paul's preceding antitheses (4:10) and repetition (4:11–12a). Like the antitheses these formally symmetrical pairs create an expectation in the readers that encourages their assent to Paul's assertion. Paul leads the readers to

anticipate that in any oppressive circumstance—his series implies
extensiveness—apostles do not claim the power to retaliate in kind.
In this last series of repetition Paul has introduced a syntactical
variation that counters the readers' potential weariness at the ac-
cumulation of repetition. At 4:12b–13 Paul shifts from a polysyndetic
to an asyndetic style, suppressing all conjunctions. The usage of
asyndeta has its own force—it characteristically heightens the dramatic effect of a passage as well as giving a staccato-like accent to the
units so "connected"—yet, in relation to the preceding polysyndeta,
it functions to create "attentional novelty."[8] At the point the readers
begin to tire of the list of afflictions and its monotonous punctua-
tion—*kai. . .kai. . .kai. . .*—Paul changes style and entices them
with another pattern.

As with the case of Paul's antitheses, his use of repetition clearly
marks the text as an instance of symbolic speech. Highly connotative, Paul's repetitions nuance weakness in terms of its extensiveness. Where his language of affliction denotes the hardships of
peculiar conditions, his repetition of those hardships connotes their
breadth and pervasiveness. Without ever saying so directly, Paul
indicates that weakness permeates apostolic existence, recurring in
various but concrete ways.

In its repetition Paul's language of affliction blocks the path to
detachment and forbids comfortable abstraction. The language of
affliction, in a certain sense, mirrors the experience which it would
depict. Paul batters his readers with this language, hitting them over
and again with repeated images of affliction that have been com-
pressed to explode rapidly in a small amount of textual space. Before
they can withdraw, Paul assaults his readers with a flurry of affliction
images whose force is, in effect, to afflict. The rapid alternation of
images, especially in the polysyndetic, unpaired series of hardships
(4:11–12a), deprives the readers of the comfort of adjusting to any
one of them or gaining distance from their force through settled
interpretation. Paul compels the reader to experience and respond
to the text without the chance to retreat to any familiar rationality.

---

[8] On the effects of asyndeton see Blass and Debrunner, #460. Ancient rhetoricians were reluctant to endorse the use of asyndeton as appropriate to literary
discourse but were keenly aware of its forceful, dramatic effect. As Demetrius
commented on asyndeton, "Thus disjointed, the words will of themselves force a
man to be dramatic even in his own despite" (*De Elocutione*, #194). Accordingly, the style becomes closely allied with the stage and with agonistic contexts.

Imagery

Through the use of concrete images in 4:9–13 Paul gives perceptible form to apostolic existence. He communicates to his readers
the affliction it entails by parading before their eyes given images of
its presence. Nowhere in this text does he set out to give more
information about apostolic affliction or to explain its meaning and
significance conceptually. By leaving the images to speak for themselves the apostle invites his readers to glimpse the contours of
apostolic existence through the markers of their own experience,
through images that can be grasped only in terms of some experienced world. Paul incites his readers to call to mind the concrete
experiences of hunger, thirst, exposure, beatings, wandering, and
labor and thus, also, to activate a sense of their associations and
connotations. The appeal to the readers' imagination causes them to
follow a different route than would be occasioned by a more abstract
diction. In that case, the readers might retreat from themselves to
think conceptually about weakness or attempt to locate it within
their familiar rationality. But in this case, no such retreat is possible.
The readers cannot understand Paul's images apart from bringing
into play their own sense of human experience, their own sensitivity
to the experience of hunger, thirst and the like.

Paul effectively uses many images to convey the affliction of
apostolic existence. Perhaps the strongest of these occurs when he
likens apostles to the world's *perikatharmata* and to the *peripsēma*
of all things (4:13). These images, virtually synonymous in meaning,
bear a root signification of "scum," "refuse," or "offscouring." Literally, *perikatharma* signifies the filth removed when cleaning something; *peripsēma*, that which is wiped off or cleaned out. The usage
of these terms prior to Paul shows the extension of the root meaning
to express personal contempt and abuse and, within cultic settings,
to signify the meanings of cleansing the community or that which is
to be thrown out after purification (e.g., an expiatory scape-goat)
(see Hauck, Staehlin). Through its root meaning this imagery gives to
Paul's weakness a repulsive reality which his readers must confront.
The hyperbole—"the refuse *of the world*, the offscouring *of all
things*"—only accents the force of an already strong cluster of images. Here Paul's imagery exceeds the force of any plain speech
statement about the scandalous character of his weakness. In the
imagination of his readers, that reality is not simply thought about,
but sensed. As with Paul's use of antithesis and repetition, so does

his imagery give heightened connotation to his weakness—here something contemptible—and draws on the readers' own experience as a factor in the perception of that insight.

The Language of Affliction: Connotation and Presence

The rhetorical situation calls for Paul to involve his readers in the connotations of apostolic weakness. Where effectively utilized, symbolic speech initiates such an involvement and sets in motion Paul's rhetorical strategy: to awaken his readers' imaginations so that they are both jolted out of familiar continuities and incited to perceive new insight into their human situation.

Connotation

Paul Ricoeur, in writing of symbolic language, notes the capacity of certain symbols to express a "surplus of meaning" or an "excess of signification." He writes,

> Freud's treatment of little Hans' wolf signifies more than we
> mean when we describe a wolf. The sea in ancient Babylo-
> nian myths signifies more than the expanse of water that can
> be seen from the shore. And a sunrise in a poem by Word-
> sworth signifies more than a simple meteorological phenom-
> enon. (1976:55)

The reader of Paul's language of affliction confronts such a surplus of meaning. For Paul, "weakness" in all its diverse occurrences has become a symbol that always exceeds its simple denotation. Its expression shimmers with connotation and estranges the notion from its ordinary contexts of meaning.

At no time does the language of affliction lose its denotation, but in 4:9–13 the sheer abundance of imagery and contrasts eclipses that dimension of the text. The swelling of forceful and imaginative language enables Paul to shout "weakness" at great volume—so much so that he makes it hard for any readers to concentrate on what he is saying without being diverted by the fact that he is speaking so loudly. When read from the vantage point of plain speech the text seems meager and redundant and, moreover, fails to account for the volume that yet rings in the readers' ears. Paul's readers know well what to do with "weakness" when spoken ordinarily, but their customary patterns of reading are unsettled by this explosion of language. The intensity, strength, and quantity of Paul's language of affliction estrange "weakness" from its ordinary associations. Recoiling from the force of the language Paul's reader cannot construe "weakness" in any ordinary way. The volume suggests the extraordinary.

Paul's forceful style brings to the surface certain connotations of weakness. First of all, the strength with which he speaks of affliction and the extent that he dwells on it imply its basic importance to his perspective. Weakness concerns Paul fundamentally and cannot be banished to the periphery of his convictions nor seen as one issue among others of equal importance. Second, Paul's literary devices freight his style with connotation. The antithetical expression of affliction, implies that, distinct from other phenomena, weakness cannot be subsumed under any and every perspective. Through repetition Paul implies that this weakness is extensive and characteristic of apostolic life. When he writes hyperbolically of affliction he suggests its radical and extreme character. Bound to vivid images weakness shows a concrete character as something which occurs within the world.

The connotations Paul gives to weakness are not inevitable, but reflect choices of rhetoric and style. For instance, if Paul had used an abstract diction he would have made weakness into a disembodied reality remote from the readers' experience of the world. If he had focused on only one hardship he would have implied that weakness occurred only within some isolated circumstance instead of pervading apostolic existence. If he had avoided hyperbole for the sake of realism he would have emphasized the ordinary, worldly dimensions of weakness but also would have obscured its extremity.

An author creates connotation through the juxtaposition of a symbol with other images that may stand in parallel or in contrast to it. A fresh connotation is expressed when a writer estranges an image from its customary associations and qualifications and sets it in relation to new and different ones. Paul's literary devices, in their capacity for juxtaposition, participate in the creation of connotation. But the context of a passage may also generate a nexus of association by introducing certain constraints and intentions which themselves bear connotation. In our text an estrangement of weakness begins with its mention within the apologetic context of argument. Where the connotations effected by Paul's literary devices yield nuance and implication, the contextual connotation penetrates deeper to the underlying value of weakness. Paul's appeal in his own behalf to the weakness God has assigned him freights that weakness with a positive value: it commends Paul's apostleship. Given the Corinthian rationality, Paul's marriage of apostleship and weakness could only seem to be at odds with his intent to defend his authority. The surprising strategy risks the readers' rejection of Paul's case but, at the same time, begins to set weakness apart from what it had been assumed to be.

By its centrality in Paul's defense weakness becomes a more perplexing matter than it had been within the Corinthian system of value. It makes no sense for Paul to claim power through powerlessness; but, in its non-sense, he has confounded that rationality and contributed to the definition of weakness. Whatever weakness may be, it is *not* what Corinthian convictions would make of it. Neither the apologetic context nor the images of weakness are extraordinary in and of themselves. Still, their combination upsets the expectations a reader would have of either of them. Bound together, their tight association unties the lines to familiar moorings and suggests that the ordinary constraints of interpretation—notably the assumed continuity between power and strength—may no longer apply. The setting of the language of affliction in the apologetic context compels the reader to seek new insight into the expressed "weakness" and its positive connotation.

Presence

One of the central functions of rhetoric is the selection and presentation of certain elements in such a way that they become vividly real in the consciousness of the reader or hearer. Chaim Perelman speaks of this function as a "making present" or as the creation of presence (1969:115–120; 1982:33–40). He writes,

> It is not enough indeed that a thing should exist for a person to feel its presence. . . Accordingly one of the preoccupations of a speaker is to make present, by verbal magic alone, what is actually absent but what he considers important to his argument or, by making them more present, to enhance the value of some of the elements of which one has actually been made conscious. (1969:117)

Similarly, Richard Vatz has noted, "Rhetors choose or do not choose to make salient situations, facts, events, etc. This may be the *sine qua non* of rhetoric: the art of linguistically or symbolically creating salience" (154). As these rhetoricians suggest, something may exist in the midst of an audience and yet go neglected by them. The power of rhetoric's "verbal magic" is to select such elements, making them unavoidable in the consciousness of the audience. Paul's self-description achieves this rhetorical effect, making apostolic weakness "present" to the consciousness of the reader.

According to Perelman, one establishes rhetorical presence by acting directly on the audience's sensibility, engaging their emotions and imaginations (1969:117 and 1982:35). Emphasizing repetitions, accentuation, and detail and using demonstrative pronouns and the present tense increase the rhetorical presence of any item so expressed. Most powerful, however, is the rhetor's use of specific, concrete diction. Where abstraction causes a concern to appear distant, the use of vivid language causes that concern to come near and to remain fixed in the audience's mind.

What occurs rhetorically in the creation of presence is comparable to the effect of Antony's waving Caesar's bloody tunic before the Roman populace: the concrete image makes the matter of Caesar's violent death present to the audience in a way which surpasses any general description of the deed.[9] An audience may, on the one hand, hear about the murder and give assent or dissent to the description all the while remaining unmoved by the report. However, when they confront the concrete image that impresses the scene unforgettably in their consciousness they may find themselves experiencing repulsion, horror, or sorrow. The concrete image ties the event to something that the audience experiences and thus insures its salience in their imaginations.

Like Antony's brandishing the bloody mantle, Paul parades apostolic weakness before the eyes of his audience. Forsaking second-order description, he forces his readers to witness specific manifestations of weakness: hunger, thirst, exposure, beatings. He etches weakness upon their imaginations and gives it an immediate presence through his forceful and imaginative style. In doing so he brings weakness into the readers' world—not just any world, but that near world they call to mind in their reading—and makes its claim unavoidable. Moreover, he brings not just any weakness for, through their reading, they themselves come to know the reality of apostolic weakness. At least in that real world of their imagination,

[9] The example is Perelman's (1969:117).

the weakness Paul brings is their own, the weakness which binds both apostle and community to the realities of the cross and the divine call to salvation. Struck by the presence of weakness, Paul's readers stand vulnerable to the force of his irony and the power of his paradoxical gospel.

Chapter V

A CONCLUDING POSTSCRIPT

> That was a way of putting it—not very satisfactory:
> A periphrastic study in a worn-out poetical fashion,
> Leaving one still with the intolerable wrestle
> With words and meanings.

T. S. ELIOT, "East Coker"

THE IRONY OF AFFLICTION: RHETORICAL EFFECT

Writing and reading are fraught with risk. Insofar as a work's meaning occurs in the interaction *between* author, text, and reader, neither the creator nor the recipient of a text can control its interpretation. Like the parent of a child, a writer gives birth to a creation that takes on a life of its own. The text's progenitor must surrender it into the keeping of others, readers who will share in the shaping of its meaning. The influence of these significant others, however, is itself constrained by the possibilities of the text. No simple puppet in the hands of readers, a text invites their reading, but always affects the reading that occurs. Within the world of the text, readers become vulnerable to the suggestions of its voice. The risk: both writers and readers may be surprised by what occurs through the collaboration of the other.

We have emphasized how Paul seeks to surprise his readers in order to bring about a basic change in their orientation. Paul, too, however, may have been surprised or at least frustrated. Convictions die hard and rhetorical strategies, no matter how well implemented, can go astray or fail to persuade. As evidenced by the continued Corinthian correspondence, the controversy over Paul's authority does not cease with the writing of 1 Corinthians. In certain respects, it only worsens.

Subsequent episodes of the Corinthian conflict lie beyond the scope of this study. If the aggravation of Paul's Corinthian relations comments on the dangers of irony, it has little authority to determine the rhetorical effect of the discourse. As we have pursued it, the rhetorical effect consists of the commitments implied if one were to be convinced by Paul's discourse. If one took seriously Paul's irony what claims would it make and what decisions would it call for? The rhetorical effect represents a potential actualization of the text and reflects the changes Paul would hope to effect in his audience as he perceives them to be.

As a summary, we will describe the potential actualization of the text in terms of three dimensions of the rhetorical situation. First, the irony of Paul's discourse serves his *apologetic* task. The paradoxical irony of 4:9–13 takes away the ground of Corinthian criticism by compelling his audience to reinterpret the very categories through which they have challenged his authority. In the world which Paul's text discloses, weakness no longer signifies simply powerlessness or the absence of God, but the presence of divine power. When caught in his irony, the critics of Paul's weakness become witnesses in his behalf.

Second, Paul's irony leads the Corinthian readers to view their calling in a new way and thereby fulfills his *homiletic* goal. Paul's irony encourages the Corinthians to affirm the worldliness of their calling, especially in its features of powerlessness. The world, no unclaimed scandal, should not and cannot be fled for it exists as the present arena of God's activity to save. As such, Paul's description of affliction becomes an emblem of the Corinthian calling no less than of his apostleship. His irony provides the vantage point from which they perceive God's identification with their weakness and the illusion of their assumed strength.

Third, Paul's ironic system of value commits his readers to basic *convictions* about the activity of God and a way of knowing reality. Theologically, Paul's convictions focus on God's vindication of human powerlessness in its myriad forms. With the cross as its essential paradigm, God's activity etches the mark of irony in human experience. Where God acts paradoxically one can know reality only with an openness to surprise, for things are no longer simply as they appear to be. The way of paradoxical irony affirms that God and the reality of the world are greater than our expectations of them.

A THEOLOGICAL PARTING

Theology cannot avoid the forge of human affliction. More than any other utterance the cry of misery haunts the theologian's mind,

rattling reminders of dogma's impotence and the hubris of knowledge. Too personal a reality to elude, too unsettling an encounter to
comprehend, the mystery of suffering robs theology of its dry assertion and plunges it deep into the ooze of human experience. There,
where fragile persons live and die, theology discovers the question
which makes urgent its search for understanding.

Paul's irony of affliction keeps before the theologian "the still
unredeemed concreteness of the human world in all its horror"
(Buber 166–67, alt.) and allows no escape from the gravity of human
scandal. Whether theology starts with a crucified god or a groaning
creation, its task to interpret human life in a created world begins
with a Pauline concession: suffering exists. That elemental fact of
suffering nails theology to a world where life and death commingle,
where the condition of being human welcomes birth at price of
mortality. In this crucible of human experience theology gropes in
the dark and learns first hand the boundaries of its language. Neither the word of enthusiasm nor futility lies open to a theology of
affliction. But between the naivete of cheap confidence and the
arrogance of despair spans a more generous irony. The world which
hosts the intimacy of life and death demands theology to speak
through paradox and allows it to do so in good faith.

Aware of the irony of affliction, theological discourse must respect the existence of suffering, but neither condemn nor glorify its
circumstance. On the one hand, weakness cannot and need not be
eradicated from the world as some enemy of human life. Tied to the
condition for life itself, weakness is a given of human experience and
may bear a preciousness about which no one should presume. On
the other hand, nor can one seek affliction as a treasure, a source of
"strength" to hoard and barter with or, as a means to power, impose
on another. Caught in paradox, the theologian can confirm the
existence of suffering, but must resist sponsoring its presumptuous
conquest or promotion. Wherever crusade masks offense at weakness
and zeal for suffering in oneself or another harbors a vengeful
idolatry, theologians must articulate the critical implications of Paul's
paradox. Forbidden to say "yes", they must speak the prophet's
"no".

The negative way of paradox yields no priestly assertion with
power to fix the place of affliction or the presence of God. It founds
no religious program to domesticate the crisis of suffering or to
liberate the afflicted from their circumstance. Still, protest may
affirm. When hurled with paradox, the prophet's "no" invokes a

vision of a larger reality, itself elusive, yet near in the irony of human experience. That ironic vision sets the afflicted free, not from the existence of suffering, but from the fear of its assumed meaning: the expectation that human plight drives away the presence of God and the communion of human beings; the dread that in our dying we are alone, cut off from life. An ironic theology of affliction moves the question of suffering away from the fact of its existence and toward its interpretation. There irony assaults the alleged certainties that threaten the sufferer with estrangement, that deep affliction within suffering which only a new vision can address.

Paul's text communicates such a vision. Inseparable from its paradoxical language, his discourse leads "weak" readers to a "threshold of otherness" (Wheelwright 21–24) where a new horizon eclipses the lure of familiar worlds of meaning. On that horizon the scandalous God appears, drawing near yet remaining other. In text, Paul brings the reality of divine presence into the readers' world; with paradox, he guards divine mystery and protects the hiddenness of a God become intimate. The near side of this reality a scarred apostle enacts as the irony of affliction. The far side of the same reality offers us, Paul's readers, the vision of a transcendent God.

WORKS CITED

Abrams, M. H.
1971   *A Glossary of Literary Terms.* 3rd ed. New York: Holt, Rinehart and Winston.

Barrett, C. K.
1968   *The First Epistle to the Corinthians.* Harper's New Testament Commentaries. New York: Harper and Row.

Bartchy, S. Scott
1973   *Mallon Chresai: First-Century Slavery and the Interpretation of 1 Corinthians 7:21.* SBLDS 11. Missoula, MT: Scholars Press.

Barth, John
1972   *Chimera.* New York: Random House.

Barthes, Roland
1967   *Elements of Semiology.* A. Lavers and C. Smith, trans. New York: Hill and Wang.

Beker, J. Christiaan
1978   "Contingency and Coherence in the Letters of Paul." *Union Seminary Quarterly Review* 33: 141–51.

Berger, Peter
1961   *The Precarious Vision.* Garden City: Doubleday.

Betz, Hans Dieter
1972   *Der Apostel Paulus und die sokratische Tradition.* Beitraege zur historischen Theologie 45. Tuebingen: J.C.B. Mohr (Paul Siebeck).
1975   "The Literary Composition and Function of Paul's Letter to the Galatians." *New Testament Studies* 21: 353–79.
1979   *Galatians.* Hermeneia. Philadelphia: Fortress Press.

Bitzer, Lloyd F.
1968   "The Rhetorical Situation." *Philosophy and Rhetoric* 1: 1–14.

Bjerkelund, Carl J.
  1967   *Parakalo: Form, Funktion und Sinn der parakalo-Saetze in
         den paulinischen Briefen*. Bibliotheca theologica Nor-
         vegica 1. Oslo: Universitetsforlaget.

Blass, F. and A. Debrunner
  1961   *A Greek Grammar of the New Testament and Other Early
         Christian Literature*. Robert Funk, trans. 10th ed. Chi-
         cago: University of Chicago.

Bleich, David
  1978   *Subjective Criticism*. Baltimore: Johns Hopkins.

Booth, Wayne C.
  1961   *The Rhetoric of Fiction*. Chicago: University of Chicago.
  1974   *A Rhetoric of Irony*. Chicago: University of Chicago.
  1978   "The Pleasures and Pitfalls of Irony: Or, Why Don't You
         Say What You Mean?" In *Rhetoric, Philosophy and Liter-
         ature: An Exploration*. Don M. Burks, ed. West Lafayette:
         Purdue University.

Borgen, Peder
  1965   *Bread from Heaven*. Leiden: Brill.

Bormann, Ernest G.
  n.d.   "Rhetorical Criticism and Significant Form: A Humanistic
         Approach." In *Form and Genre. Shaping Rhetorical Ac-
         tion*. K. Campbell and K. Jamieson, eds. Falls Church,
         VA: The Speech Communication Association.

Brandt, William J.
  1970   *The Rhetoric of Argumentation*. New York: Bobbs-Merrill.

Buber, Martin
  1961   *Two Types of Faith*. N.P. Goldhawk, trans. New York:
         Harper and Row.

Bultmann, Rudolf
  1910   *Der Stil der paulinischen Predigt und die kynisch–stoische
         Diatribe*. FRLANT 14. Goettingen: Vandenhoeck und
         Ruprecht.

Carpenter, Ronald
  1976   "The Ubiquitous Antithesis: A Functional Source of Style
         in Political Discourse." *Style* 10: 426–41.

Conzelmann, Hans
1975   *1 Corinthians*. J. Leitch, trans. Hermeneia. Philadelphia: Fortress Press.

Cuddon, J. A.
1977   *A Dictionary of Literary Terms*. Garden City: Doubleday.

Dahl, Nils A.
1977   "Paul and the Church at Corinth." In *Studies in Paul*. Minneapolis: Augsburg.

Deissmann, Adolf
1911   *Light from the Ancient East*. L. Strachan, trans. 2nd ed. London: Hodder and Stoughton.
1957   *Paul: A Study in Social and Religious History*. W. Wilson, trans. 2nd ed. New York: Harper and Brothers.

Dempster, Murray W.
1980   "Rhetorical Logic in Ethical Justification: A Critical Exposition of Chaim Perelman's 'New Rhetoric.'" Ph.D. dissertation, University of Southern California.

Doughty, Darrell J.
1975   "The Presence and Future of Salvation in Corinth." *Zeitschrift fuer die neutestamentliche Wissenschaft* 66: 61–90.

Eco, Umberto
1976   *A Theory of Semiotics*. Bloomington: Indiana University.

Eliade, Mircea
1959   *The Sacred and the Profane*. W. Trask, trans. New York: Harcourt, Brace, and World.

Farrar, F. W.
1879   "The Rhetoric of St. Paul." *The Expositor* 10: 1–27
1885   *The Life and Work of St. Paul*. New York: E.P. Dutton.

Fish, Stanley
1972   *Self-Consuming Artifacts*. Berkeley: University of California.
1980   *Is There A Text in this Class?* Cambridge, MA: Harvard.

Fitzgerald, J. T.
1984   "Cracks in an Earthen Vessel: An Examination of the

Catalogues of Hardship in the Corinthian Correspondence." Ph.D. dissertation, Yale University.

Frei, Hans
1974   *The Eclipse of Biblical Narrative*. New Haven: Yale.

Fridrichsen, Anton
1928   "Zum Stil des Paulinischen Peristasenkatalogs 2 Cor. 11:23ff." *Symb Osl* 7:25–29.
1929   "Peristasenkatalog und Res Gestae." *Symb Osl* 8:78–82.
1944   "Zum Thema 'Paulus und die Stoa.'" *Coni Neot* 9:27–31.

Frye, Northrup
1957   *Anatomy of Criticism: Four Essays*. Princeton: Princeton University.

Funk, Robert W.
1966   *Language, Hermeneutic, and Word of God. The Problem of Language in the New Testament and in Contemporary Theology*. New York: Harper and Row.

Gibson, Walker
1980   "Authors, Speakers, Readers, and Mock Readers." In *Reader-Response Criticism*. J. Tompkins, ed. Baltimore: Johns Hopkins.

Goodman, Nelson
1978   *Ways of Worldmaking*. Cambridge: Hackett.

Greimas, A.J. and J. Courtes
1982   *Semiotics and Language: An Analytical Dictionary*. L. Crist, D. Patte, et al, trans. Bloomington: Indiana University.

Guettgemanns, Erhardt
1966   *Der leidende Apostel und sein Herr*. FRLANT 90. Goettingen: Vandenhoeck und Ruprecht.

Harvey, Van
1969   *The Historian and the Believer*. New York: Macmillan.

Hauck, Friedrich
1965   "Perikatharma" in *Theological Dictionary of the New Testament*. G. Kittel, ed. and G. Bromiley, trans. Grand Rapids: Eerdmans.

Hawkes, Terence
1977 *Structuralism and Semiotics.* Berkeley: University of California.

Heschel, Abraham Joshua
1966 *God in Search of Man. A Philosophy of Judaism.* New York: Harper and Row.

Holmberg, Bengt
1978 *Paul and Power. The Structure of Authority in the Primitive Church as Reflected in the Pauline Epistles.* Coniectanea Biblica, New Testament Series 11. Lund: Gleerup.

Hurd, John Coolidge
1965 *The Origin of 1 Corinthians.* New York: Seabury.

Iser, Wolfgang
1975 *The Implied Reader.* Baltimore: Johns Hopkins.
1978 *The Act of Reading. A Theory of Aesthetic Response.* Baltimore: Johns Hopkins.

Jakobson, Roman
1960 "Closing Statement: Linguistics and Poetics." In *Style and Language.* T. Sebeok, ed. Cambridge, MA: M.I.T.

Jervell, Jacob
1976 "Der schwache Charismatiker." In *Rechtfertigung.* J. Friedrich, W. Poehlmann, and P. Stuhlmacher, eds. Tuebingen: J.C.B. Mohr (Paul Siebeck) and Goettingen: Vandenhoeck und Ruprecht.

Judge, E.A.
1960–61 "The Early Christians as a Scholastic Community." *Journal of Religious History* 1:4–15 and 125–37.
1972 "St. Paul and Classical Society." *Jahrbuch fuer Antike und Christentum* 15:19–36.

Kaesemann, Ernst
1969 "On the Subject of Primitive Christian Apocalyptic." In *New Testament Questions of Today.* W.J. Montague, trans. Philadelphia: Fortress Press.

Kermode, Frank
1980 *The Genesis of Secrecy.* Cambridge, MA: Harvard.

Kierkegaard, Søren
1968   *The Concept of Irony with Constant Reference to Socrates.*
        L. Capel, trans. Bloomington: Indiana University.

Knox, Norman
1961   *The Word IRONY and its Context. 1500–1755.* Durham,
        NC: Duke University.

Krentz, Edgar
1975   *The Historical-Critical Method.* Philadelphia: Fortress
        Press.

LeGuern, M.
1978   "Elements pour une histoire de la notion d'ironie." In
        L'Ironie. Linguistique et Semiologie 2. Lyon: Presses Uni-
        versitaires de Lyon.

Levertov, Denise
1961   "Three Meditations." In *The Jacob's Ladder.* New York:
        New Directions.

Liberman, M. M. and E. E. Foster
1968   *A Modern Lexicon of Literary Terms.* Glenview, IL: Scott,
        Foresman.

Lynch, William F.
1973   *Images of Faith. An Exploration of the Ironic Imagination.*
        Notre Dame: University of Notre Dame.

McFague, Sallie
1975   *Speaking in Parables. A Study in Metaphor and Theology.*
        Philadelphia: Fortress Press.

Mackey, Louis
1971   *Kierkegaard: A Kind of Poet.* Philadelphia: University of
        Pennsylvania.

Malherbe, Abraham
1977   *Social Aspects of Early Christianity.* Baton Rouge: Loui-
        siana State University.

Meeks, Wayne A.
1983   *The First Urban Christians. The Social World of the Apos-
        tle Paul.* New Haven: Yale University.

Meyer, Paul W.
  1965 "Some Aspects of Tradition and the Problem of its Control within the New Testament." A paper presented at a joint meeting of the Biblical Theologians, The Society for Theological Discussion, and the Duodecim, November 12–13, 1965.
  1979–80 "The This-Worldliness of the New Testament." *Princeton Seminary Bulletin* 2:215–31.
  1981 Review of *Galatians*, by Hans Dieter Betz. *Religious Studies Review* 7: 318–23.

Muecke, D. C.
  1969 *The Compass of Irony.* London: Methuen and Co.
  1970 *Irony.* Critical Idiom Series, vol. 13. London: Methuen and Co.

Mullins, T. Y.
  1962 "Petition as a Literary Form." *Novum Testamentum* 5: 46–54.

Munck, Johannes
  1977 *Paul and the Salvation of Mankind.* F. Clarke, trans. Atlanta: John Knox.

Niebuhr, H. Richard
  1963 *The Responsible Self.* New York: Harper and Row.
  1974 *The Meaning of Revelation.* New York: Macmillan p.b.

Patte, Daniel
  1976 *What is Structural Exegesis?* Philadelphia: Fortress Press.
  1980 *Paul's Faith and the Power of the Gospel. A Structural Introduction to the Pauline Letters.* Philadelphia: Fortress Press.

Patte, Daniel and Aline Patte
  1978 *Structural Exegesis: From Theory to Practice.* Philadelphia: Fortress Press.

Perelman, Chaim
  1979 *The New Rhetoric and the Humanities. Essays on Rhetoric and its Applications.* W. Kluback, ed. and trans. Synthese Library, volume 140. Dordrecht, Holland: D. Reidel.
  1982 *The Realm of Rhetoric.* W. Kluback, trans. Notre Dame: University of Notre Dame

Perelman, Chaim and L. Olbrechts-Tyteca
  1969 *The New Rhetoric. A Treatise on Argumentation.* J. Wilkinson and P. Weaver, trans. Notre Dame: University of Notre Dame.

Petersen, Norman
  1978 *Literary Criticism for New Testament Critics.* Philadelphia: Fortress Press.

Plank, Karl A.
  1981 "Resurrection Theology: The Corinthian Controversy Re-examined." *Perspectives in Religious Studies* 8: 41–54.
  1985 "Confronting the Unredeemed World: A Paradoxical Paul and His Modern Critics." *Anglican Theological Review* 67: 127–136.

Ricoeur, Paul
  1970 *Freud and Philosophy: An Essay on Interpretation.* D. Savage, trans. New Haven: Yale University.
  1975 "Listening to the Parables: Once More Astonished." *Christianity and Crisis* 34: 304–308.
  1976 *Interpretation Theory: Discourse and the Surplus of Meaning.* Fort Worth: Texas Christian University.
  1977 *The Rule of Metaphor. Multidisciplinary studies of the creation of meaning in language.* R. Czerny, trans. Toronto: University of Toronto.
  1981 *Hermeneutics and the Human Sciences.* J. B. Thompson, ed. and trans. Cambridge: Cambridge University Press.

Robinson, James M. and Helmut Koester
  1971 *Trajectories through Early Christianity.* Philadelphia: Fortress Press.

Schneider, Norbert
  1970 *Die rhetorische Eigenart der paulinischen Antithese.* Hermeneutische Untersuchungen zur Theologie 11. Tuebingen: J.C.B. Mohr.

Scholes, Robert
  1974 *Structuralism in Literature: An Introduction.* New Haven: Yale University.

Scholes, Robert and Robert Kellogg
  1966 *The Nature of Narrative.* New York: Oxford University.

Schrage, Wolfgang
1974 "Leid, Kreuz und Eschaton. Die Peristasenkataloge als Merkmale paulinischer theologia crucis und Eschatologie." *Evangelische Theologie* 34: 141–75.

Schuetz, John Howard
1975 *Paul and the Anatomy of Apostolic Authority.* MSSNTS 26. Cambridge: Cambridge University.

Staehlin, Gustav
1965 "Peripsema." In *Theological Dictionary of the New Testament.* G. Kittel, ed. and G. Bromiley, trans. Grand Rapids: Eerdmans.

Suleiman, Susan and Inge Crosman (eds.)
1980 *The Reader in the Text. Essays on Audience and Interpretation.* Princeton: Princeton University.

Tannehill, Robert
1975 *The Sword of His Mouth.* Semeia Supplements 1. Philadelphia: Fortress Press and Missoula, MT: Scholars Press.

Taylor, Mark
1980 *Journeys to Selfhood: Hegel and Kierkegaard.* Berkeley: University of California.

Theissen, Gerd
1982 "Social Stratification in the Corinthian Community: A Contribution to the Sociology of Early Hellenistic Christianity." In *The Social Setting of Pauline Christianity.* J. H. Schuetz, trans. Philadelphia: Fortress Press.

Tompkins, Jane P. (ed.)
1980 *Reader-Response Criticism. From Formalism to Post-Structuralism.* Baltimore: Johns Hopkins.

Vatz, Richard E.
1973 "The Myth of the Rhetorical Situation." *Philosophy and Rhetoric* 6: 154–61.

Vielhauer, Philipp
1974–75 "Paulus und die Kephaspartei in Korinth." *New Testament Studies* 21: 341–52.

Weiss, Johannes
   1897   *Beitraege zur Paulinischen Rhetorik*. Goettingen: Van-
          denhoeck und Ruprecht.
   1970   *Earliest Christianity, A History of the Period A.D. 30–150*.
          F. C. Grant, trans. Gloucester: Peter Smith.

Wheelwright, Philip
   1968   *The Burning Fountain*. Bloomington: Indiana University.

Wilckens, Ulrich
   1968   "The Understanding of Revelation within the History of
          Primitive Christianity." In *Revelation as History*. W. Pan-
          nenberg, ed. and D. Granskou, trans. New York: Mac-
          millan.

Wittig, Susan
   1975   "The Historical Development of Structuralism." In *Struc-
          turalism. An Interdisciplinary Study*. S. Wittig, ed. Pitts-
          burgh: Pickwick Press.

Wuellner, Wilhelm
   1970   "Haggadic Homily Genre in 1 Corinthians 1–3." *Journal of
          Biblical Literature* 89: 199–204.

Zmijewski, Josef
   1978   *Der Stil der paulinischen "Narrenrede." Analyse der
          Sprachgestaltung in 2 Kor. 11, 1–12, 10 als Beitrag zur
          Methodik von Stiluntersuchungen neutestamentlicher
          Texte*. Bonner Biblische Beitraege 52. Koeln-Bonn: Peter
          Hanstein.

Zyskind, Harold
   1979   "The New Rhetoric and Formalism." *Revue Internationale
          de Philosophie* 33: 18–32.

INDEX OF SUBJECTS AND MODERN AUTHORS

Fridrichsen, Anton, 5
Frye, Northrop, 37
Funk, Robert, 2

Gibson, Walker, 9
Goodman, Nelson, 63
Greimas, A. J. and J. Courtes, 8

Harvey, Van, 7
Hauck, Friedrich, 85
Hawkes, Terence, 8
Heschel, Abraham J., 72
Holmberg, Bengt, 17–18
homily, homiletic, 12; context (of 1
  Corinthians 1–4), 24–30
horizon and theme, 50, 54
Hurd, John C., 15, 23

imagery, 85–86
imitation, 23
irony, 3, 5, 10, 33; as conviction, 64–
  67; definition of, 34–42; detection
  of, 44–45; and dissimulation, 36–
  37, 38–39 (see also dissimulative
  irony in 1 Cor. 4:9–13); in Greek
  and Roman tradition, 35–36; as
  instable, 67–69; Kierkegaard and,
  42–44; and nothingness (nihilism), 44, 67–68; paradoxical,
  39–42 (see also paradoxical irony
  in 1 Cor. 4:9–13); as Protean, 34–
  35; as second perspective, 37–38;
  as way and method, 68–69
Iser, Wolfgang, 8, 50–51, 52–53

Jakobson, Roman, 8
Judge, E. A., 75

Kaesemann, Ernst, 28
Kermode, Frank, 54, 59
Kierkegaard, Søren, 42–44, 62, 67,
  68
klēsis, 26
Knox, Norman, 35
Koestler, Arthur, 37
Krentz, Edgar, 7

language: of affliction, 3–7; symbolic, 1, 71–73

LeGuern, M., 36
Levertov, Denise, 81
Liberman, M. M. and E. E. Foster,
  37
literary criticism: and textual context, 11; study of Paul, 2–3
literary-rhetorical paradigm, 7–8
logos, 18–19
Lynch, William, 40

McFague, Sallie, 2
Malherbe, Abraham 75
Meeks, Wayne A., 18
metalanguage, 18, 20
methods, literary and rhetorical, 7–
  9
Meyer, Paul W., 12, 28, 29
Muecke, D. C., 34, 35, 36, 43
Mullins, T. Y., 23
Munck, Johannes, 15

New Rhetoric, 8
Niebuhr, H. Richard, 21, 73
nihilism, 67–69

parables of Jesus, 2, 62
paradox: definition of, 40; in 1 Cor.
  1:18–31, 55–58; as instability, 67–
  69; irony of, 39–42; as system of
  value, 64
paradoxical irony in 1 Cor. 4:9–13,
  51–62; appropriation of 1 Cor.
  1:18–31, 55–62; and textual
  blank, 59–62
paradoxical knowing, 64–67; and
  Corinthian controversy, 66–67
paradoxical system of value, 62–69;
  as instable, 67–69
parakalō, 23
Patte, Daniel, 3, 7, 8, 23, 63, 72
Patte, Daniel and Aline Patte, 1, 8,
  71
Paul: authority of, 18–20; and the
  eschatological reservation, 28;
  imitation of, 23; and Jesus, 2; and
  judgment, 13–14; as poet, 1–3,
  12; and symbolic speech, 75–77;
  travel plans of, 14–15; weakness
  of, 15–16 and passim

INDEX OF BIBLICAL TEXTS CITED